Nest

Nest

Letting Go from Italy, France & Ireland

Jennifer McGuire

IGUANA

Publisher: Meghan Behse
Editor: Paula Chiarcos
Front cover design: Ben Ren

ISBN 978-1-77180-485-1 (paperback)
ISBN 978-1-77180-484-4 (epub)

This is an original print edition of *Nest: Letting Go from Italy,
France & Ireland*

Before you read this book, please remember, memory is not a perfect science. It is slippery and changeable and, sometimes, just plain wrong. I have written this tale from my memory and I have tried my best to do justice to everyone included.

I have changed people's names and details where I thought it was appropriate.

If I have mentioned you in this book, know that I love you so very much. Any mistakes made are mine alone.

Toothpaste on the Mirror

Nobody tells you how many times your kids die. Maybe not every year but at least every three. More when they're little. This is what kicks me in the stomach in the washroom this morning.

I'm standing in front of a sink with zero beard hairs clinging to the chipped silver drain. My toothbrush holder has one that's mine only and two that have gone mouldy from being forgotten. This can happen to toothbrushes and also people, but I'm not going down that dark lane just yet.

It's tough enough to stand here and look at my oval mirror and see there are no toothpaste spit dots along the bottom. The hand towel I hung yesterday in the ring beside the sink is still there, the towels folded neatly in threes instead of crumpled on the floor or — and this is what I always find worse — hanging weird. Boys don't know how to hang towels. I think this is from their Neanderthal days when they didn't have towels but only grass or plain outside air to dry themselves. Every time Nathan had a shower I'd go in after him and sigh loud enough for him to feel it and take his extra damp towel off the shower hook where he tried to hang it by balling it up and jamming it in place. I hung it over the shower curtain rod every time, thinking maybe this time he'd get it.

Now my towels are all hung neat. The window is two-thirds open so there's a breeze for when I'm in the tub. When they were little, I'd take a long bath at night with that window open and candles and wine and Billie Holiday singing "He's Funny That Way" in my ear as though I was a pretty big deal. Then I'd hang around waiting to tell someone about my night because it felt like a sexy vignette I should share.

In my bathtub there are still signs of the boys who are gone. Axe body wash that's empty enough to leave behind but not full enough to ever use. This is the same with every peanut butter jar, ketchup bottle, jam jar.

I wish I didn't need to tell you about this because it's the most boring cliché, until it's your everyday life then, oh brother, is it irritating. Almost as irritating as the smell of Axe mingled with teen-boy sweat that gets in your clothes no matter how many times you wash them. Maybe Axe is the smell of our life together.

My four sons and I have lived in many houses during our sixteen years alone. All rented and all a little nicer than we could afford. Now when we talk about the early years, we identify our houses by address and smell.

The first place we lived in when we left my husband, armed with toys but no washer or dryer or enough beds, was on 9th Avenue in my hometown. This place smelled like diapers and Aveeno oatmeal bath treatment from that time they all got chicken pox together. Also, cookies. All our houses smelled like chocolate chip cookies on account of me needing to apologize to them through batter so often. The next house was haunted for sure and smelled like dust and mouse shit. That was my darkest year. After that we found the little place on 3rd Avenue that was supposed to be someone's part-time cottage but became our full-time home.

It smelled like scented candles in a revolving menu of pumpkin spice for fall, cinnamon apple for winter, and mango and tart raspberry for summer. Also *Toy Story 2* bubble bath, crock-pot chili and, finally, laundry soap. Finally, we could do laundry in a house of our own.

Axe was the smell of our 7th Avenue East house, the one with the good upstairs *and* the good downstairs. The only place where everyone had their own bedroom — do the math — that means a five-bedroom house. If I were going to add a photo to this book, it would be a crayon map of that house. Nathan liked to draw it when we lived there; it was bigger than anything to him. It was all windows and had two fireplaces but also green carpet — because it was just a rental and no one was giving us good hardwood floors, obviously.

Ben was in his young teens when we lived on 7th Avenue East and he really liked the ladies. He was hoping the Axe body spray would get them to like him back. He played football that year, learned the drums and the guitar. Plus, Ben was becoming big-man handsome instead of young-man pretty in those days, so things were looking up. I wasn't sure if the Axe helped but I can tell you, our towels and dish cloths and sheets and even my bras that were washed with Ben's clothes had that spicy testosterone Axe smell in them for years after.

Ben is now a grown man with his own apartment and a girlfriend (no more Axe). The same with his older brother, Callum, living in Toronto in a basement apartment with twinkle lights and potted succulents and a girlfriend of his own who wears red lipstick and plays the ukulele. Ditto Jack, working in an office with benefits and business-casual khakis like he's forty because he always forgets he's just twenty and so does everyone else but me. I'll always remember his age for him. Nathan is in his first semester at university to become a history teacher. This will be a good job for him. I already know this. He's taught me more about history than any teacher ever with his excellent blend of knowledge plus passion plus relating everything to movies I've seen.

I figure this Axe bottle is from Nathan. He never really smelled like Axe or anything other than Nathan when he was still here sleeping down the hall, but I think he was just more subtle than his brother. I wonder if I should keep it for him when he comes home. I wonder when he's coming home. I wonder if he still thinks of this last rental like it is his home. The stone house in the country that smells only like me and my containers of salad with more blue cheese than lettuce. It doesn't feel like my home. Even though the pear picture is hanging in the kitchen right now. The pear picture is supposed to be the sign that we're home. It's just a generic print I bought for thirty dollars when I was first on my own with the boys, but it's become our hallmark for knowing *we are home*. Every time we had to move out of a house we couldn't afford and left our smells behind, and sure, a garbage bag or two, the pear picture came with us.

After we were told to move out of the darkest house by our darkest landlords, Callum (who was about twelve) caught me sitting in my room sobbing. It wasn't hard, I was pretty loud. He came in to ask me what was wrong because that kid was never an asshole at all, and I said I was sorry with words and not cookies. I was so sorry that we were moving again. So sorry that I never got anything right. Sorry that he'd just finished hanging his posters in his room and now they would come down and he'd have to start all over again. He said this to me — I remember every word — "It's okay. We know you'll find us a good place. You always do. Wherever the pear picture hangs is our home." Which had always been true until now. It turns out I'm homeless without my boys. The pear picture is just a print I don't want to look at anymore. I am rootless. All those years when I was looking for the love of my life, guess what? They are the loves of my life and now they're gone and I'm left standing in this clean washroom clutching an Axe body wash bottle staring at my face that's blank as anything. I might have raised them up good but I forgot to raise me up too.

I think of all the versions of them who have died before this final death. Of five-year-old Callum wearing that red polar-fleece vest and navy t-shirt and khaki pants every day. Of him coming home from school to see baby Jack, soft and pink and sweet, and loving him so much he cried. Saying to me, "Why does he always want you? Doesn't he know I'm his brother?" This is a Callum I'll never see again. He is dead forever.

So is six-year-old Ben. Wearing his Hawaiian shirt over a t-shirt to school for the lip-sync battle he won effortlessly with his rendition of "All Star" by Smash Mouth. Where he whipped off that shirt and threw it into the screaming crowd of grade-school children for effect. He signed autographs late into recess and said to a furious Callum, "Don't worry, you have talents too but they just don't show like mine." This Ben is gone for good.

So is four-year-old Jack. Wearing a tie and a *Ben 10* watch to his first day of preschool and carrying his backpack like a briefcase. So confident and brave until nighttime when he needed to sleep beside me with the little light on.

Nathan at three. Asking a cashier at Walmart if maybe she's a hundred and pointedly coughing if someone smoked a cigarette near him and waking me up every morning with a hand on my face to tell me I'm beautiful. I'll never see him again no matter what. It's all over forever and this final death of the people they were has turned out to be the death of us as a group, and this is the thing that takes away all my breath.

I don't know when I decided to run away to Europe like a real tacky jerk. Maybe I decided that twenty-five years ago, when I was a young mom of twenty-one, huddled in some apartment with my first baby boy, Callum, and a side order of disappointing partner. Even then I knew deep down it was never going to be a clear road for me. I knew I'd need an endgame. I don't know exactly when the idea of Europe became a physical thing, when I stopped scrolling through towns in Italy and France and Ireland like it was a TV show I was half watching and became the director of instead. I booked a flight and carried around a screenshot of my Airbnb in Italy on my phone to show people, like it was a baby photo anyone cared about. I booked flights for all the boys to visit too, even though I'm pretty sure they just wanted to start being their own people instead of just a piece of the pizza that was always us.

I'm packing up the pear picture. I'm hoping my friends throw me a party. I'm even leaving a good man behind to wait for me in the log cabin he built with his hands. Or not wait for me. I don't know.

All I know is I can't stay here without them. Maybe I can't be anywhere without them.

A Wife and Three Childs

There are more discount stores in Italy than I thought because maybe I thought there would be zero. Maybe all my knowledge is from two movies (*Under the Tuscan Sun* and *Roman Holiday*) and one HBO series (*Rome*). Not once did I ever think of Italian people needing to buy plastic cutlery or a six-pack of Bic pens, and this is my first disappointment as I'm driven alone in the back of a ten-person shuttle bus from Leonardo da Vinci Airport to Tivoli, where I'll live for January and February.

Along the highway there are discount stores and gas stations and big-block apartment buildings that look like all apartment buildings beside highways. I could be in Mississauga for all I know. It's dark but for all the discount stores and casino lights, maybe around 10:00 p.m., but I can't be sure, I'm so tired. The kind of tired where I could just sleep in this shuttle with a stranger driving in a foreign country, and I do. It's been more than twenty-four hours since I left the kids back at the airport — three sons and two girlfriends and Starbucks coffee cups in our hands as one girlfriend snapped a photo of our family. *Almost* our whole family — because our baby Nathan was back at school and we said our goodbyes that morning. I left him with clean laundry and a little bit of money that probably wasn't enough. I could feel it in my ribcage how it probably wasn't enough. I could feel all the ways he'd be trying to budget for the week until I was paid again: the noodles he'd eat, the socks that would need to be replaced, but he isn't at the age where he thinks socks need to be replaced. I hugged him when I left, a panicked hug. My fingers were claws and it was the kind of hug where we both tried not to cry and we clung a little. We both felt scared for ourselves and maybe a little bit for each other. We broke apart and he said, "That was awkward," and everything should have felt better but, of course, it didn't. I was still leaving.

I just couldn't remember why.

At the airport it was the same. Ben and his girlfriend, Jess, had asked to borrow my car. I reluctantly agreed but noticed on the snowy ride to the airport that the tires felt weird and it was making a clunky sound that felt like about $600. I told him and he said, "It's fine. We'll figure it out," but Jess looked worried. She didn't want to figure it out, she wanted to feel safe. Outside Lester B. Pearson, a January storm was settling in at 10:00 p.m., thick and furious. Ben was going to use my car to drive everyone home after I left, and when I said goodbye at the gate, all I could think was, *If something happens, I won't even know for at least twelve hours.* Then, *If something happens, I won't be able to come home right away.* And finally, *If something happens, it's going to be my fault.*

On the plane I stared out the window at the wet snow coming down sideways and freezing so fast that we had to wait on the tarmac so the wings could be de-iced. Most of my children were driving in my car with my twenty-two-year-old son who maybe thinks he knows more about driving than he really does. He doesn't have snow tires on that car. This was the thing that went around in my head until I landed in Lisbon for my four-hour layover and could finally access Wi-Fi again. The thumbs-up sign from Ben didn't fill me with any kind of relief. Instead, I just thought, *Four months to go.*

When I booked my flight to Italy, I booked the cheapest one possible and didn't realize it would take over eighteen hours of travel to get from Toronto to Rome. More than that because my flight from Lisbon to Rome was delayed. I didn't think about how I'd get myself from Rome to Tivoli because, when I was scrolling through potential Airbnb listings at home in Canada, Italy felt about the size of my thumbnail. I assumed trains would run from my front door to the trattoria of my choosing. I assumed there would be express trains from the airport directly to Tivoli, and I'd meander down a street or two to my lovely new studio with my luggage clicking on the cobblestone behind me.

I don't know why I thought this, especially since I lived in a tiny village called Echandens (just outside Lausanne in Switzerland) for a year when I was nineteen. For a year I lived by train schedules and then my thumb and then rides from friends who were impossibly international. That year in Echandens was probably the reason I decided I needed to go to Europe when my sons were grown.

When I graduated from high school, I found out that I couldn't head off to university because I was too poor, so I went to Europe instead. I was an au pair with my best friend, Gina, and we took off for Switzerland. At first, I hated it and then I never wanted to come home. This is the thing you should know about my life there. I became me when I was there — a me that wasn't already picked out by my mom or my aunts or my grandparents or my friends. I was exactly no one in Lausanne and this suited me down to the ground.

I came home and got pregnant straight away by a boy I didn't love, and the person I was in Switzerland became this new person called Mom. Then Mom and Mom and Mom again. Always more Mom than anything else. This is why I figured I'd head on back to Europe. It was the place where I figured out how to become me before, and now I'm here hoping I'll figure it out again.

Only this time, I see casinos and gas stations on my first night, alongside dollar stores, and I wonder why I left people who need me for this place. I'm tired and I've been wearing the same socks for so long I don't know if they'll ever smell like regular socks again. I'm older than I was, older than I've ever been. I realize it suddenly, like it's something that has only happened to me.

Fabrizio the driver is whispering on the phone to his girlfriend as he drives me to Tivoli. He needn't bother hiding his love chats, my Duolingo has already totally failed me with my Italian and I can't understand a thing. He's a friend of my Airbnb landlord, Renato, whom I contacted in a panic from Lisbon when my flight was delayed and I was worried there wouldn't be any more trains to Tivoli. He told me the train would cost me about €11 and the walk to the studio from the station in Tivoli would take about fifteen minutes, but maybe it would be too difficult for me at this time of night? Instead, he'd send his friend Fabrizio (who has a car) and he could pick me up for €80. So around $130. A huge chunk of my spending for the month, but I said yes because I was carrying four months' worth of luggage after flying and waiting in airports for longer than an entire day.

I said yes but I sort of felt like Renato should be picking me up as a favour. Even though I was a stranger renting a studio from him for two months, I still thought he should do this for me. He didn't agree.

The drive to Tivoli takes about forty-five minutes, so longer than the "ten minutes outside Rome" that Renato initially advertised. I'm glad to tell you that the closer we get to Tivoli the fewer dollar-store-with-casino-plus-gas-station combos I see. There are more old buildings, washed a kind of greyish white with age. Thin winding streets, too narrow for cars and yet here we are in a car. We whizz down my road (in what is called *the Ancient Quarter*) and park at the end of a cobblestone courtyard with its own fountain and everything.

Fabrizio doesn't talk to me but he does grab my suitcase in one hand while smoking, this I appreciate. He sees Renato and calls out, "*Eh, ciao, ragazzo!*" that translates in my Duolingo to *hello, little boy*. Renato comes shuffling over, a short round man maybe a few years older than me who looks like a cartoon Italian chef. Round eyes, big nose and a bowling pin of a build. He greets me with kisses and takes me away so Fabrizio can count my money. That's €80 gone and I'm not happy about it; my envelope had only €300.

My studio is behind one of the hidden doors in the courtyard of stone buildings. I don't see it at first behind the life-sized nativity scene still outside my door in January. When I point it out to Renato in a way I know feels like I'm mocking it (because I am), he smiles stiffly and says, "Yes, we're Catholic" just like that. Already he's deciding not to like me. *I'm Catholic too*, I think, *but the bad kind who doesn't like church.* So I don't say anything.

I try again to be friendly when I see my room, a stone-wall studio he calls *the cave*, which would be charming if there was a window or something. It is charming. I decide it's charming with the stone floors and stone walls and old door featuring the one tiny window behind curtains that will almost always stay closed because this is where I'm going to do all my living for two months. Renato lives upstairs but there are so many versions of "upstairs" here, this could mean anything. The courtyard is full of windows of different people's upstairs. I tell him I love the room. I love the little pellet stove giving off a cheerful warmth. I love my big white bed that takes up most of the room, my tiny kitchen fitted with exactly enough of everything for two people maximum. Two knives, two forks, you get the picture.

Renato loves that I love this, but when I ask him if there's somewhere close to buy something for my dinner because I haven't eaten since that one custard tart at the airport in Portugal, he frowns. "It's all closed, everything. In Tivoli it's all closed." I ask him if there's somewhere to get a slice of pizza and this is, apparently, also not possible but he makes a suggestion. "I can bring you some food to here. Do you want wine?" When he says this, I lunge at him like I'm going to kiss him. I'm hungry and dirty and desperate, yes desperate, for a glass of wine. He backs away and says, "I have a wife and three childs." He hustles out the door to get the food and leaves me there feeling like a failed sexual predator until he brings me a root-vegetable soup, a bit of bread, some sort of meatball and cheese and sautéed greens, plus a cold bottle of dry white wine. I thank him in English because I forget. He says, "You need to learn Italian if you stay here," and with a stony face, he leaves me alone with my food. It's fine though. I have enough for a party, even if it's going to be a party just for me.

I have enough for now.

The Schoolyard

When I left Canada for Italy, there were no parties for me. I don't know what I expected but I guess you could say I expected a party. But I'm the one who throws the parties mostly. My boyfriend, Nick, and I threw parties at his log cabin in the woods (the place where I lived for one year a few years ago and moved out because it wasn't right). Nick and I have been together for four years or so. I met him when I tried to run a local literary magazine called *The Tin Roof Press* and he was part of an artists group interested in running an ad in my summer edition. We were a bad fit on paper from the start. He's twenty-two years older than me, no children and one marriage from many years ago, which he remains vague and remote about. Nick is an old hippie with a car that looks broken but drives like a dream. He's a laid-back massage therapist, an artist who likes to make whirligigs of Stompin' Tom Connors (whom he refers to as a "national treasure" and don't even bother arguing), and he paints watercolours of forests and houses and pretty girls he knew before this pretty girl right here. He's been a musician since forever, which is probably why he's so confident. Most mornings Nick wakes up and looks at himself in the mirror (with his sticking-up salt-and-pepper hair and his lean body and his sparkly eyes), grins and says, "Hey, not bad for an old guy."

Nick was meant to be a summer fling. This was the thing I told everyone but me. "He's so wildly inappropriate obviously." I liked saying this best, like I was always the decider. Sure, he was wrong for me. I probably told him he was wrong for me too but he's been deaf in one ear since childhood so he didn't listen. He knew before me that we were right in more ways than we were wrong. The sex was good, the kind of sex that made me feel easier to be around. I learned how to be naked with Nick (a skill I didn't know I needed) and forget about my skin. He never thought we were a fling. Loved me right away and wrote notes about me in his day timer with my name and smiley faces and everything. And when I finally decided I might love him too (after a few months of fighting myself), he smiled his good smile and said, "It's about goddamn time."

Living together with the kids wasn't in the cards for us. His log house was too tiny and too remote. When I moved out, everyone sort of figured that would be the end and so did I. I'm still not sure if that wasn't the end. I remember when he asked me to move in with him and said to me, "It's perfect, you finally get a home and I finally get a family." My friends and I cried over how beautiful that was, really so lovely. Except, it turned out, it wasn't my home and it wasn't his family. I was writing a screenplay for a movie only I wanted to watch.

Still, we stayed together, we were together. I thought we were together. I lived in my rented house close to the beach just outside of my hometown of Owen Sound, but when we had parties it was always at the cabin. Pizza parties where I made everyone bring a topping and put their pie together themselves, Pictionary parties, Oscar parties, you name it.

Somehow, we just forgot to have a going-away party for me. Nick thought it would be down to my friends, and they thought it would be down to him, but we all know it should have been down to me. We know our roles, and party planner is mine, all mine.

Sylvia, Bev and Laura are some of my oldest friends in Owen Sound. They were the moms I ran to when I was raising my boys and didn't have their dads to run to for advice. There were seventeen children between us. We understood each other and we mostly liked each other's kids, especially now that they were all grown (and not beating each other up in the schoolyard). The Schoolyard Moms was what the teachers called us. The last ones to leave at the end of the day, letting our kids play together on the equipment and on the grass for hours after school let out. Not a one of us interested in going home to cook meals for people who didn't always appreciate our efforts or clean up after people who should maybe — yes, definitely — know how to clean up after themselves.

We started out in the playground, lingering in the yard under the shade of a willow tree until someone's husband would slowly drive by wondering if he should start dinner or wait a little longer ("Five minutes," someone would say — like it was ever really five minutes). Eventually our friendship moved to shopping and camping and nights at the local pub for half-priced appetizers and drinks before a movie. Then breakfast on the first and last day of school, a tradition of eggs and coffee and maybe pancakes too (the good blueberry-ricotta ones at the Dragonfly Café).

I was always the last to leave, always. Because I got to be a regular mom with them. When Bev said, "I'm taking the kids out to a movie and dinner tonight. I cannot deal with dinner," I'd nod like that was something I could do too. And

I could, once I saved up all my kids' free movie coupons from Nesquik cereal and Lucky Charms and also those free popcorn coupons from El Paso taco kits. Once I managed that, we'd bide our time until a really good movie came out (or even settle for one of the *Spy Kids* in a pinch) and take a six-dollar taxi armed with my careful stack of cardboard cereal-box cut-outs. And for the night we were regular.

I liked nodding along with Sylvia, discussing her menu for the weekend with friends and family popping over, like this was the most normal thing — to be able to feed people turkey dinners or coffee cake or bottles of wine from a well-stocked liquor cabinet. I nodded like, yep, me too. That was me all over again.

And the weekends came, the ones without the boys and without friends, when I should have been living life but instead I lay on the couch getting fatter and fatter. Growing out my pubic hair like it was a choice. Alone and alone.

The weekends weren't for friends like me. Friends shaped like a question mark. The weekends were for first-tier friends and all tiers of family, for busy happy lives everyone pretended they wanted to escape, but they knew better. Mostly they knew better. They knew if they walked away from those lives, they would become me.

Laura knew and understood me. We didn't talk about it, but she knew I was alone. She knew why I didn't want to go home to a past-due notice for the gas bill on the door. She'd say, "Come to my house" for dinner or a movie or game night, and we did, all of us. She let me pretend for as long as I wanted. Pretend I wasn't alone.

She knew not to ask the questions that started coming at me from all sides when I made the big decision to leave. Getting my hair coloured at the salon before I left, a young mother of three asking, "Why Italy? Why France? Why now?" Her face saying *What's the rush?* Maybe she should have been asking, *Why the multi-toned caramel highlights? They'll be impossible to maintain for four months.* "Who will watch the kids?" — from a woman from school who wore seasonal brooches even though I didn't believe we'd hit our brooch years yet. "What about your career?" — from my sister-in-law with the great job. "How are you going to afford this?" — from every friend who called me out of the blue.

My mom didn't ask, "What's the rush?" but all her questions were *Why now?* adjacent. "What about Nick? What if he meets someone else? What will you do if you run out of money? What will you do about your car, your friends, that mouse living in your cupboard, the kids, the kids, the kids?"

I had answers for most of their questions. My landlady was giving me a break on the rent while I was away. She never said why but I thought she understood. She's a single woman who survived cancer and now owns a little cottage at the beach and a Mini Cooper and three sweet dogs. She knows about choosing her own path. I work from home as a writer for a parenting site so my work was coming with me. Affording was going to be a struggle, a stretch. I had rented tiny studios by the month since they offered a 50 percent discount. I knew how to live cheaply. This, at least, no one questioned. Only one question felled me, asked by everyone, "Won't you be lonely?"

Won't I be lonely?

I wake up late in Tivoli. There's no coffee in the studio and I forgot to brush my teeth last night so I can still taste the bottle of wine I drank. I barely slept. It was too quiet. It was the wrong kind of silence, the kind where I knew I was in the wrong place even when I drifted off a little. The building I now call home was built in the fifteenth century (a time a person from Canada can't fathom) and the walls are thick. After a few hours of lying in bed listening to the pellet stove slowly burn its way through wood chips that smell like the kind guinea pigs have in their cages, I put the TV on. It was almost all Italian TV, loud and colourful with laugh tracks, a game show of some kind. I've slept with the TV on at least ten thousand times in my life. When the kids were little and visiting their dads for the weekend, it was usually something on Citytv or a cartoon if they were home. The white noise of a TV was as soothing as a lullaby for most of my life, but I couldn't do it with this last night, I couldn't get the volume right. It would start off quiet, just some foreign lull in the background, then suddenly someone would screech or yell or laugh and wake me up.

It's around one in the afternoon. I missed my first morning in Italy entirely. I feel like I already disappointed an audience I didn't know was going to be watching. Like I'll have nothing to report at the end of the day. Why did I make such a big fuss and leave? Why?

There are no schoolyard moms here. No one to save me from myself. No friends at all.

Breakfast in Tivoli

My first morning in Tivoli isn't actually morning. It's one o'clock, something I didn't learn from the dark cave of my studio in this village on the outskirts of Rome until I checked my phone. The jet lag is bad, worse than I expected, but I have a job to do and this job is making memories. So, no sleeping for me.

I have to pick my way through the rabbit warren streets of charming cobblestones, cold and slick in January, to find a café. Here I'll become the swirly new European version of me. I'll write and take my morning coffee and sit, becoming part of the fabric of this ancient place. This tiny version of Rome with a chip on its shoulder and laundry hanging just about everywhere.

I walk and walk. I wear clothes in dark colours that are almost right but still a bit wrong. Too plain, too North American, too clearly from Old Navy. Every café I pass is called a bar. Men stand at counters in cashmere scarves taking shots of espresso. A few people glance my way. *I don't fit*, I think. *I'm blonde and curvy, middle-aged and afraid.* But also, I think, *I don't fit* yet.

The café I find is bright and happy looking with pale grey-and-white shiny glass counters stuffed with croissants and doughnuts and little pistachio-covered tarts. Also cannoli. That always makes me want to say, "Leave the gun, take the cannoli," because quoting *The Godfather* in Italy is cliché but fun. I see a bag of chips I don't recognize, paprika flavour. I wonder who decided paprika chips should be a flavour when they're obviously just watered-down barbecue. Imagine munching on chips, pausing and waiting for a burst of something that never comes — and now you know what paprika chips taste like, a whisper of a chip.

It's early days here, of course. I'm struggling with the loss of my kids and my friends and my routine and I'm feeling a bit maudlin. But I'm going to live in Europe for four months, like I've been longing to for the past twenty years, so expectations are running high. Too high on account of too many rom-coms maybe.

I order my coffee with the only sentence I know in Italian, "*Uno caffè latte, per favore*," and I'm met with a disinterested stare from the Italian model/barista behind the counter, telling me with her eyes she doesn't have time for tourists today, and I'm telling her with mine she can go ahead and make time because this is happening. We have a standoff. I get my coffee and then realize I'm also very hungry.

In Canada, I'm a breakfast eater. One of those people who has several breakfasts, in layers. First, a healthy green smoothie and coffee. Then a hike outside, where I think about the next breakfast and make my plan of attack, savoury or sweet or a mix? Back at home, with red cheeks and good intentions, I pour more coffee and snack on a piece of toast with cheese and honey while making my main-event breakfast. This will be a soft-boiled egg (salt and pepper on every bite, please) with a second piece of toast, final coffee, reading glasses and a crossword. On a cold day it's oatmeal with berries, coconut, apple, cinnamon and maple syrup with a book in my favourite chair by the good window. On Sundays, when no one is working and we have miles of time, pancakes and sausages stacked high with my sons around the table, syrup and laughter everywhere. My breakfast wears many coats.

In Italy, breakfast looks like this: shooters of espresso and a *cornetto*. Just like a coffee and a fancy croissant, basically. That's it, no variety. Also, I'm telling you this as a public service, if someone in Italy tries to sell you a chocolate croissant, they mean Nutella, which isn't chocolate. I'm fooled by this one too many times. On my first, I don't know that's all I'll get for breakfast. I think I might as well treat myself to a croissant, and surely, I'll find some fruit later. But in January in Italy, there are only clementines and old apples. I love a clementine but they're not to be trusted with their hidden seeds. Eventually I find a grocery store with six-packs of eggs in the back, like a speakeasy, and these are the most delicious eggs I'll ever eat, but they never boil right for me. Either the yolks are too hard or the whites too runny. Pancakes have to wait, as will my delicious sons, whom I left at home to go about being grown-ups without me for four months. Fruit in the supermarket is expensive. Tiny boxes of blueberries that cost me four euros (nearly six dollars) for one portion, and I pop them like pills.

I keep going back to this café alone, drinking my caffè latte and sitting at a table and writing. No one ever speaks to me. They know I'm doing it wrong. And I wonder if there will ever be a *yet*.

After a while, I make friends who introduce me to the true main event of eating in Italy: pasta carbonara. We explore and drink wine, locals teaching me how to be local. Hike to little villages in the mountains and eat and eat. I learn the way. But every day I also wake up feeling the roller-coaster drop of my stomach before my eyes open. I'm not where I should be. Every day I feel the painful loss of my morning ceremony and my not-so-bad-after-all life at home. I miss my sons. And yet I'm here. For the next four months, I get to be a new person because nobody knows the old person.

Pancakes can wait.

A Pile of Rocks

I meet Tim four days into my stay, but we're already bantering email friends. Tim is a Canadian, a writer, a friend of a friend with an impossibly glamorous job working for the European division of a big newspaper. My friend Michael introduced us since he was worried I'd be alone. I was worried about forcing myself on people, but it turns out this is nothing new to Tim or his wife, Karen. They are used to giving up Sunday afternoons for people who need to learn Rome. Karen works as a translator. They aren't my class of people or maybe I'm not their class of people, but our mutual friend is their class of people and he loves me, so they invite me over for an afternoon of coffee. Their apartment is in a good residential district in Rome close to the Colosseum and the Circus Maximus that I see as soon as I got off the Metro like it's no big deal. It's just standing there for anyone to look at with their plain old eyes.

Tim's apartment is on the B line of the Metro that I find pretty much fine. I believe it's considered the more genteel of the Metro lines with the A line being the place to get pickpocketed but also the way to all the touristy things. People on the A line either have hard faces or itineraries; on the B line, it's bags of groceries and covert napping. I like it because it's easy to navigate, no getting lost. This is surprising and refreshing after being lost in Tivoli for two hours my second day there. My Google Maps wouldn't work in a town with such tightly wound streets or maybe it won't work in a town so old. All I know is that after a while every house looked the same. Mellowed gold, laundry hanging out the window, red flowers on stoops and big heavy doors. If not for the centre of town, I'd still be lost today.

I find Tim's apartment on a leafy side street just behind the United Nations building, and let me tell you, there should be a movie about his place. I'd watch a movie filmed here for sure. I'm pretty certain I'm in one already. Inside, full beams of natural light stream through tall windows onto books and heavy, expensive furniture that gets used all the time, you can tell — it isn't just for show. The movie version of this apartment stars a woman of a certain age living there writing her manuscript after a lifetime of ill repute. Wearing silk robes and writing longhand by real fireplaces, her hair in a tight bun or down long and wild and grey — this apartment needs someone like that. Instead, it's inhabited by Tim and his family, who are six shades above regular, but regular nonetheless. He invites me in with his floppy hair and his height and his scarf, like he's Gregory Peck. His face, like he was bored of me already. Like we've been friends for twenty years and he's had enough. His wife, Karen, is curled up on some mid-century deep-green velvety sofa wearing expensive layers of ochre linen that could be pants or a dress or a tunic or a onesie. Impossible to tell from any angle. She half smiles and offers me coffee.

"Oh, that's okay, I'm good. I don't want to put you to any trouble." She assures me it's no trouble and then insists. When I relent, she brings me into the kitchen to watch her make my coffee so I can see it is for sure so much trouble. Karen does this thing with her eyes called not blinking, and as she makes coffee, her lips are in a half-smile that feels worse than a frown. I see in her face that she doesn't want me there. I see in her face she wants me to see this but we say nothing about it. We take my coffee back into the massive living room to get down to the business of acting. Acting like expats who would like each other even if we lived in, oh I don't know, Hamilton.

Tim joins us. We make the smallest of talk. They speak a different language from me, the language of people who have done big things. They've seen places outside these apartment walls. I suspect they have a bathtub here, which I already know is rare in Italy. They tell me they looked up my writing online, and I blush because now they know I'm a fraud. A writer for a parenting site who covers breaking news about celebrity pregnancies. Not a foreign correspondent who has earned the right to their filmy scarves.

But Karen says, "I saw your article about your sons. You raised them on your own?" I say yes, and she gets real for a minute, shifting her ochre layers to lean forward. "That's really remarkable, you know. Really." I shrug and she says, "I can't even imagine." No one can even imagine, ever. This is what I hear constantly. But Karen says it in a way that's wistful, like maybe she wants to imagine.

I ask her about her kids and she tells me she has two daughters, one who just flew back to Montréal for school. She gets the faraway look I know from all my staring into the bathroom mirror.

"It's hard, isn't it?" I ask.

"Well, yes, you know, it is. It really is. It just feels so quiet here without her. She left this morning and I didn't even think I could look in her room for a while. I didn't know."

I tell her to give it time, like I know what I'm talking about. Tim interrupts to ask about our mutual friend who works for the prime minister and is a big deal. I don't have much to offer in the way of political gossip since we're friends by way of our small town, but I pretend. "Oh, he's a real character, isn't he?" Then Tim looks at his watch and offers to take me out on his Vespa for a tour of the city. I say, "No, it's too much trouble," like you're supposed to, but he ignores me. He needs to check me off his to-do list so that he and Karen can have their dinner in peace.

I ride on the back of his Vespa in my mini gloves and warm coat to the top of the Aventine Hill where there's a fragrant orange grove and a view of the whole city, all rooftops and river and light. We ride to the neighbourhood of Trastevere, where he tells me Cleopatra once slept as she hid in the city so no one would know she was there as Caesar's mistress. We move on to the Piazza Navona for pizza but it's too busy, full of tourists watching puppet plays and eating roasted chestnuts as they enjoy the Feast of the Epiphany, the last hurrah of Christmas in Italy. We drive on by the Castel Sant'Angelo on the banks of the Tiber River (so fast I can't catch my breath). Whizzing by cars, I almost hit my knee on someone's rear-view mirror. Tim is showing off how brave he is, but I'm not so brave. It's too fast, too much, too exciting, too everything all at once. I don't know enough about anything so I don't know what to be happy about yet.

Tim really knows everything. He grew up here as a young boy and returned as a man. He takes me to a good pizza spot and explains the authentic places don't have seats, you just stand at the counter. Also, the good spots sell you slices by the pound and cut pizza with these special scissors. He shows me a gelato place where they give money to fight the Mafia that I thought didn't exist outside of the movies. He tells me how to avoid pickpockets (carry very little and use the inside pockets of your coat) and reminds me that you can eat lunch only between twelve and two since everyone closes in the afternoon — things people who have travelled already should know, but he knows I don't know anything, so he tells me. He's nicer than I expected. When we stand in front of the statue at Campo de' Fiori, he offers to take my picture, and when I say no, he says, "Give me a break here, you know your kids will want one."

On the back of Tim's Vespa, I start to relax, a muscle at a time for every personal story he tells me, every small moment of humanity where he lets me in, past his rakish good hair and good leather jacket. He tells me about his battle with cancer, about how he and Karen came to parenthood late in life and were worried they weren't quite getting it right. I want to tell him no one gets it right, but what do I know? I'm not even here all the way in Rome with him, not really. I'm back in my bedroom at home, setting my *SpongeBob SquarePants* alarm clock for 7:15 a.m. on a Wednesday to get the kids out the door for school. I might never leave that place.

After a while I tune back into the show I'm writing with Tim in Italy, and I play a gentle soundtrack in my head as we whip through the cars, something instrumental and sleepy. He shows me that spot from *Roman Holiday* where Audrey Hepburn watches Gregory Peck put his hand in the lion's mouth to see if he was telling the truth — we both just really love that scene. We watch the sun go down over the Tiber from the Vespa. *Slower*, I think, but maybe it's because I'm not expected to look at everything so hard now that I'm seeing it all for the first time. The ripples in the river. The arch of the bridges. The pink light on everything.

Tim tries to teach me about Rome but I'm not so great at listening. He knows. He tells me I should learn a little something about the history of Rome, or else I'll just be "walking around looking at a pile of old rocks."

After the sun goes down, we stop at the supermarket to pick up some food since the stores are going to be closed the next day, Sunday. We both buy cheese and pasta and prosciutto. He shows me where to find strawberries from Spain. I buy two bottles of wine without looking him in the eye. Tim takes me to the train station and says goodbye without looking back. The Circus Maximus is lit up (so is the Colosseum, though I can't see it as well from the station). Lit up from underneath, from somewhere deep within. Lit up the way a beautiful person is lit up from all their good things. Except nothing good happened there, did it?

I take the train home. Another day in the books and this one might have been good enough for Facebook. I'm excited to get home to Netflix on my laptop. I'm excited my audition as a traveller is done for the day.

Latin Lover Experience

What do you do for a living?
How did you meet your wife?
Where would you recommend I visit in Rome?
Are you an only child (emergencies only)?
Where do you live in Tivoli?

These are my questions, translated into careful and probably not-correct Italian, in my journal for Luca, the man I've slotted to be my new best friend. My lifeline, the only person outside Tim who has made sustained eye contact with me in eight days, and I'm planning on clinging to him like a sucker fish. He and his friend Francesco are guides I found via an Airbnb experience where a person can hike the mountain that overlooks Tivoli, called Monte Catillo. It was the cheapest thing I could find. I knew how to get there on my two feet and I was allowed to speak English at no extra cost. After a few days of trial and error, I had just about figured out how to get from my little place to the main area of Tivoli and also the train station. My studio in Tivoli is downhill from everything, and there are all these rules about driving on the cobblestone roads of my part of town. I think the main rule is, just don't. This means no buses run past my place and no taxis, and even if they did, I probably wouldn't know how to call one. It's pretty charming without all the cars. People come to fill jugs of water at the fountain just outside my courtyard, and they light it up at night and everything. Also, the streets are narrow and people always have clothes out on the line to dry from the apartments above, even though it's January. I like this. It makes for a good photo to share with all my two hundred or so social media friends who I'm trying to trick into thinking of me as adventurous. The pictures are especially excellent when someone parks their red Vespa below some fluttering clothes in the sunshine. My street is pulling a ten for pictures.

I meet Francesco and Luca on a cool, bright Monday afternoon for a climb up the mountain through a cork forest where we get to walk up a winding path, past lazy cows and through olive trees that smell like something lemony and sweet. The group is me and a family of four who are all varying shades of blonde. I talk a little with the sweet American family, all wearing white socks and sneakers, sunglasses and puffy vests over polar fleece. They came on holiday while their sons were off from college even though they own a holiday home back in North Carolina. The wife tells me this almost straight away. I get the feeling that the wife and two sons aren't all that happy about being in Italy, but the dad, he likes it just fine when he doesn't have to find parking. "Do you know we drove all the goddamn way to Naples and turned around after we couldn't find parking? We looked for an hour and a half and nothing, just nothing. How do these people stand it?" I tell them I don't have a car here, and they try not to say it but they think this is worse, much worse. They're getting ready to fly back home the next day so I'm ashamed to say, I don't put too much effort into them. They aren't going to be permanent.

At the top of the mountain, the entire group stops so we can catch our breath and Francesco can dole out red wine and some small biscuits (which he pronounces bisk-wits so earnestly I can't correct him). Delicious treats his mother made for all of us to enjoy as we watch the sunset together. The vista is incredible, green valleys and hills and another village in the distance sitting on top of another small mountain like this one. Luca, who started out shy with his English, tells me the village is called San Polo dei Cavalieri, a very old commune with the best ravioli you will ever taste. He tells me I can walk through the mountains by the Way of the Wolf, just a romantic name for a hiking trail. I say I'd like to try it and he says, "Do you want to have lunch there tomorrow?" I say yes immediately. This is my time to say yes, I guess.

That's why I'm sitting in my studio writing out interview questions with sweaty palms and thinking about a panicked warning from Nick: "Be careful, doll, this guy could be a real creep and look at you! You know what he's thinking." Luca tells me straight away he's married to a woman he loves. He's the kind of handsome and charming middle-aged Italian some women hope to meet here. A thick head of hair, a good strong chin, an easy smile and deep-brown eyes. He isn't thinking anything about me, I can tell. Also, I'm not thinking anything romantic about him and probably he can tell. No Latin Lover Experience for us.

This is the thing that sometimes happens when women come to Italy to meet men, I learn. Luca and I eventually learn to spot these women at once just because they look so much better than me. Carefully constructed, nervous and excited women from the United States or Norway or Ireland or New

Zealand, all looking to find something better than they found at home. Women who've been hurt maybe. Women who are tired of trying to make things work in their hometowns with their homegrown men who maybe don't appreciate them as much as they could. So why not throw caution to the wind, get on a plane and head to the land of pasta and pizza and men who love women? I understand this. It's a bill of goods we've all been sold via Hollywood and romance novels. When you feel underappreciated, go ahead and try a Latin Lover Experience. At the very least, get compliments like *Ciao, bella* or *Ciao, bambola*. These seem guaranteed. I think I might be a woman who wants this, but so far, I'm not. I didn't bring the right wardrobe. My three drawers at the studio are full of black leggings and long-sleeved t-shirts, jeans and sweaters and one dress but no heels, so I don't know why I bother. I don't have the legs for flat shoes and dresses. Not Latin Lover outfits, and besides, I suspect Luca doesn't need to chase after women. I don't say this to Nick when he frets over my lunch with Luca. We left things awfully strained and I don't know if I want to comfort him or not.

Luca and I go for lunch at a restaurant somewhere close by since the good ravioli place is closed. He drives me in his car and this part feels bad right away. Too small, too awkward, too intimate, especially when he reaches over to kiss both my cheeks like everyone does (but usually they're standing upright in the street). Maybe I should be nervous, but then we start to drive. I'm not nervous about assault, I'm just trying to stay alive.

If you remember going to the Fall Fair as a kid, and the Scrambler, the ride where you get strapped into your seat and whipped left and right and your stomach is constantly lurching because it doesn't know where to settle, you now know driving in Italy (it's the same for trains, buses, cars).

Luca tells me over and over, "I must prove to you Jennifer, Luca, he is not dangerous." He might mean in the rape way, but I'm wondering about him in the driving way.

As we drive, I try to ask him my questions, and he answers in English fairly well but kind of laughs at my list and says, "Oh, I prepare nothing. I think we just talk, okay?" And so we do. At the restaurant, he helps me choose my layers of meal and orders confidently from the waiter, and I feel so grateful for this. So grateful to have had my order taken in Italian without making anyone irritated. In just one week, I'm positive I irritated everyone with my kindergarten-level Italian, but not here. Here we eat and we talk. We talk into his phone via Google Translate. I tell him about my four sons and he tells me about his two brothers and his nephews and his parents and his wife, Angela, a woman who is a lawyer (which he pronounces "liar" and I don't correct him). They've been together for twenty years but married for three. I don't ask him extra questions about that, but boy would I ever, if my Italian were better. When I say I'm a writer, he tells me about a book he's writing; of course, it's science fiction on account of men universally loving science fiction. I tell him I don't want to be one of those tourists who don't speak Italian and we agree to try hiking together as a sort of language exchange. Already we are friends even though the only sentence I've learned in his language is "the elephants are eating the cheese" — because I wouldn't pay to upgrade my Duolingo when I was studying back in Canada. Still, we eat lunch for three hours and somehow manage. We eat food in the order that I've learned here. First plate is some meat, like veal or pork. Second plate is the main-event pasta. Dessert is usually tiramisu or small doughnuts dipped in sauce. There's always bread for dipping in olive oil and this is something you eat and eat. Picking away at it mindlessly, your wine glass always full. Bottles of wine, maybe two or three.

Later Luca would say to his friends, "Watch this. Canadian women, they drink like Italian men," and I would feel proud but also worried for a minute. We talk about the Latin Lover Experience. He tells me, "Yes, all of the women come here to have the Latin Lover but they forget, when do we work? We are tired. There's no time for the Latin Lover here. We want to go home to eat dinner, Jennifer, there is not this time for passion."

He doesn't mean his wife, Angela the liar/lawyer, whom I meet later in the day when he takes me to his apartment. They live in Tivoli but in a part that was built after World War II, in an apartment building with tall ceilings and windows, so many windows. I like Angela right away. She has acres of dark curls and wears comfortable pants. She's also shy with her English like him, but then there is this confidence. She isn't the sort of woman who wastes her time worrying about a woman like me because she knows. She knows her husband, Luca, he isn't dangerous.

We exchange numbers and I go home. I let myself be excited. For just a minute, all these feelings bubble up in me that I remember from my Friday nights of planning back in Canada. This was what I wanted. To meet people and make them like me and maybe I can like them too. Maybe we can be friends, maybe they can teach me things. I let myself think that maybe I made the right decision and maybe I can do this on my own and maybe I'll learn whatever it is I think I need to learn here. I've earned the right to do nothing tonight. A full day to mark in my calendar so I can go back to my cave where I'll have a disappointing shower and open a bottle of wine and watch season two of *The Marvelous Mrs. Maisel* and wonder why Midge's children are never around.

Sweatpants and Casseroles

I've been dreaming about the boys a lot in the past few weeks but it started in Canada before I left. With all the goodbyes, like I was never coming back, we had the big Christmas at the cottage on Georgian Bay that was rented from a friend, the one with six bedrooms and three bathrooms. I was always thinking of bedrooms and bathrooms, always space.

Everything was crystallized and important in December. Callum's girlfriend, Amy, joined us for the holidays for the first time, and her presence meant the vegans outnumbered the meat-eaters, so we decided to do a casseroles-and-sweatpants Christmas. I called it that in all our group messages, *Casseroles and Sweatpants Christmas*, but it never caught on. No one stopped me, they just didn't partake. We swapped recipes and put together a menu for our three days together. Jack made his bean-tortilla thing and Ben's girlfriend, Jessica, sent him with a vegan shepherd's pie even though she couldn't come. Callum brought a soup, Nathan brought nothing but helped me pack everything. I made four vegan casseroles and three desserts. My heart was pounding, like I was running a marathon the whole time. "Why is your face so red?" Nathan asked when he came into the kitchen once, and I told him I had no idea. My face goes red a lot since I'm one of those people who blushes, but this wasn't a blush. It was panic coming out of my cheeks. I had nowhere else to put it all. My roller-coaster ride slowly *click-clacking* its way up the hill for the first drop. I'd strapped myself in and there was no escape.

The cottage was great, apart from Nick arriving sick and miserable. It wasn't his fault, but we all blamed him for ruining our holiday. I hated him for that. I hated him for weakly limping around the cottage in his way-too-loose long johns and worn plaid robe. I hated that he was so concerned with his own sickness in the way of people who don't have kids. Feeling his own forehead for a fever with the back of his hand, giving me updates on his poor sleeping. "Just a few hours this time, doll. I'm hoping to sneak in a nap in a while and try again." Asking me over and over again if I think he should have a bath to make himself feel better. I told him that maybe he should rest at home since it was only fifteen minutes away, and he gave me one of those quavering brave faces like he'd muscle through this horrible time just for me. He stayed and stayed and stayed. I hated him then. We all did. It wasn't his fault, but there you have it.

Ben and I stayed up late on Christmas night and had a drink in the hot tub with Jack perched on the edge keeping us company. We decided to get out and make snow angels, and my pumping heart felt like it might explode with the cold. Ben called out, "Jesus, why did we think that would be a good idea?" No one knew.

That night I dreamt of him as a teenager, awkward and gangly and bullied, though he never said much about it until later. In my dream we were living in our little house on a dead-end street, the 3rd Avenue cottage, and he'd just come back from seeing his dad for the weekend. I was standing at the stove stirring a big chili for supper, and he was walking me through all the food he'd eaten at his dad's place. This was something he always needed to do though we don't know why. "On Friday night we asked him to stop at McDonald's, but he said we could wait until we got to Toronto. I had some leftover sandwich from school in my backpack so I just ate that in the car. Then when we got to his house, he made us grilled cheese and soup but he didn't have ketchup."

"Oh, hon," I said. This was the worst thing that could happen to Ben, then and now. As a little boy, he wouldn't eat anything without ketchup on it, and since I was a twenty-three-year-old kid myself when I had him, I didn't know any better, but now I guess it was too late.

"It's okay," he said. "I had some packets in my backpack from when you sent me to school with Kraft Dinner. Then on Saturday morning we went out for breakfast. That was good. I got pancakes. For dinner on Saturday, Dad barbecued ribs but they weren't very good. I didn't like them. Today we had a late breakfast, just cereal. That's why I'm so hungry." Their hunger was a physical thing I felt in my sleep and it was the beast I wanted to satisfy but it wouldn't be satisfied. In my dream I was cooking this chili and there was enough, more than enough for us all. It was a good dream.

The dreams I've been having since I got to Italy are bad. Helpless, awful, real. One dream is only this — a wave. My boys and I are at the beach, Sauble Beach on Lake Huron, where we'd gone our whole lives. The beach where my mother and her sisters and her mother and her father took me as a six-week-old baby to dip my toes in the lake. An anointing that stuck real good. In this dream of mine, Nathan is sometimes a baby and sometimes four or even five, they're all different ages. Their swimsuits I see best, Jack wearing a Spider-Man suit with a matching rash guard and even goggles, his thick dark hair wet around the edges from sweat or swimming. Cal wearing overly baggy plaid swim shorts and a sweatshirt, and I think, *Oh, this is the stage where he felt bad about his body*, like it's a movie but it doesn't feel like one. Ben in a long pair of skateboard shorts double knotted at his skinny little waist. Nathan, long-haired and sun-kissed and round-bellied, in turquoise trunks spotted with navy hammerhead sharks. They're near me and playing with a mesh bag of Dollar Store sand toys I always kept in the car. It's quiet and easy until my ears start ringing but I can't move. A tidal wave is coming for them. All of us, but really them. It casts a shadow over us, it's so high. They all stand and turn to look at me and I see their eyes, blue-grey-green like mine. And they know I can't help them. They know I'm useless. I want to wake up before the wave takes them but I never do. I just have to watch them get swept away. Every time.

They know I can't help them. And when I wake up, this is what I know too.

Not Bad for an Old Guy

Luca brings me to Rome to meet Nick at the train station. We left early to go for a long walk and parked near his parents' apartment in the San Giacomo neighbourhood where he grew up. A neighbourhood of apartments over pizzerias and small fruit markets, of parks and locals drinking coffee on the sidewalk shouting, "Ciao, Luca!" when we walk by. It's been only two weeks or so but Luca and I already have our habits. We've been walking this route alongside a cliff outside of Tivoli, which is part residential and part nature, with clear views all the way to Rome if there are no clouds. We have coffee sometimes but sometimes we don't, because it gets me too hyped up and I'm already a little too much here. "Like a cartoon," Luca tells me. "You have so many expressions, it is like you are a movie character."

In his parents' Rome neighbourhood, we stop in at his favourite bakery to eat some delicate little *cornetti* filled with a pistachio cream, Luca eating three and me eating two. We both like eating and so does Angela. She said to me once, "For me, I like to eat," and it wasn't even an apology. Not like when I went for appetizers with my friends at home, and we'd all come up with excuses for why we were hungry. Bev forgot to bring lunch to work and Sylvia hiked twice and I was getting my period, so that was why the extra potato skins made sense. This isn't the way it is with Angela, her appetite is a celebration. For Luca too and now for me, maybe, too.

Luca gets extra *cornetti* to bring back for Angela but I don't get any for Nick, because I'm nervous. Nervous because I'm not sure if we're going to end things. Nervous because I don't know if I want to end things. Nervous about picking him up from Termini. Luca takes me for a walk to visit an old church to take my mind off things and when I ask him how old this church might be, he shrugs and says, "Wikipedia" because he isn't a tour guide. I'm nervous because my new friendship, the one that felt like it was fixing all my worries in Italy, is going to go away now that Nick is coming.

By the time Nick gets to Rome at the end of January, I've forgiven him for being sick at Christmas. Even though he made me sick too, just as I was packing and trying to wrap up my layers of goodbyes with my kids. So sick I didn't wake up for twenty-four hours. Jack was home and lonely for me, I could feel it through my fever. People don't think your kids will get lonely for you when they're grown, your boys especially, but that's where they're wrong. I could feel him downstairs with a bag of chips and a movie pulled up on Netflix waiting for me to hang out with him. I was busy upstairs sweating through my pyjamas and seething at Nick. The man I was going to be breaking up with anyhow. I was pretty sure.

After a few weeks alone in Italy, I'm ready for Nick to get here for his two weeks with me. I'm not sure if I miss him or home or speaking English or someone laughing at something I say that sounds clever instead of odd. Luca did his best on our hikes, but I think I frighten him. My miming and gesturing is too big and too American for Italy, even though I'm not American. Each day I've tried speaking in Italian, and each night I've gone home with my head feeling full of cotton balls, trying so hard to grasp Italian the way people really speak it. I need to be around someone who knows I can be funny without me having to say, "I'm funny" in terrible Italian. I miss being charming because I can be very good at it when I want.

Luca tried to help me find my charm again and also gave me the regular words I needed to get through the day. The first thing I asked him was how to ask for a bag at the grocery store since the girls who worked there were losing patience, but even after I knew it was *borsa* it made no difference. They still wanted me not to be there.

I told Luca about Nick the day before he was set to arrive, on a Friday, when we were out for our language-exchange walk. I told him he was much older than me, too old really. We laughed about how it was always this way with men looking for younger women. We laughed even though my stomach hurt from this betrayal. "It is not normal for a man like this to have a woman like you. It's good for him, yes, but not for you, yes?" It wasn't as though I hadn't heard all this before, of course. From my mom and my friends and my kids with their eyes because they knew better than to say it out loud. I knew all the reasons we shouldn't be together, and yet…

I meet Nick at Termini station in Rome wearing jeans and a black turtleneck; he's basically wearing the same thing. When I see his smile, I start to cry. He kisses my hair and hugs me tight and whispers, "Thanks to God, thanks to God," even though he isn't religious. I say, "Are you crying?" to stop myself from letting it all go and he says the thing he always says, "Of course, what am I, a monster?" Something in me opens then, cracks open a little for him. Something I thought I was getting ready to close for good.

You're not supposed to care about these things, but I do, and I stand so very still in the hoop of Nick's arms, my head resting right under his chin. His hands always rest on the groove above my ass, which my sons have spoken to me about with horror. My heart slows down for the first time in weeks when he hugs me, and I'm ashamed of myself. He's supposed to be here interrupting my adventures, not saving me. I'm supposed to save me. This too was decided long before him. All of this was decided long before him.

The Train

A week after Nick arrives we get on the train in Tagliacozzo and I'm tired. I thought I was tired from trying to speak Italian all day and eating disappointing polenta and climbing, always climbing. But it's more than this. Today it's Nick and the management of him. If I want to walk to the right he says, "Let's try left instead," and we try left, who cares. When I think we should find a restaurant, he wants to find a map first and so we do. The same with lunch and then with coffee in the afternoon. All these bland little micro decisions where I'm recalculating and recalculating my route. We get on the train to go back to my studio — that is now our studio, in Tivoli — and this is where I have my meltdown.

It goes like this: I see two seats on the train, and he gently touches my arm and says, "Why don't we try the next car, it's up higher," and so I recalculate my route. The next car is full of Italian policemen. And I'm sorry to tell you I'm afraid of the police. So I start to back out, like I have fifty pounds of cocaine strapped to my person. The police laugh, and I blush — not like a schoolgirl but more like I'm full of fire and it's only coming out my cheeks. They tell me no, stay, stay, don't be silly, and then all the men laugh, and I want to blow up the train but only the parts where they are sitting. Nick, the man our friends believe to be long-suffering for putting up with all my parts, goes quiet because he knows something is up but he doesn't know what yet. I don't know what yet either, so I stare out the window and hold my breath because that will really show them all. I think about why I'm so tired and mad.

After the next stop, where two women in long black dresses with paper shopping bags full of leafy greens get on, I think I know. I look at these women who are frowning, like it's their full-time job. I think they're making the food that night for a house full of people or maybe just one person. They know what this person wants to eat, like a flesh memory, like they know all the things the people they love want to eat or wear or whatever. They know it better than anything. They don't know how to know the things about themselves anymore.

I know this because this was obviously me. When I was raising my sons and even before. Even long before when I had a mother who was the boss of everyone and she married a man who was the boss's boss. All my choices were questions answered by other people. My mom who had me when she was so young and my boyfriends who were all smart enough to keep one foot of their love out the door just in case. But mostly my sons. If we were seeing a movie, we saw something they'd want, like *The Avengers* or *Batman*, and I found a way to make this something I'd choose too. I'd find a storyline that interested me, like Captain America and Iron Man and their feud. I'd order double-butter popcorn so it wasn't like I was a martyr, don't be silly. The houses we lived in were picked based on how many bedrooms there were for the kids, and the furniture was never the Scandinavian white racket I longed for because of dogs and boys. And it wasn't like you sat around thinking about the choices you didn't get to make because it never occurred to you. You recalculated your route, and it was barely a centimetre each time, but after a while there was just no finding your way back.

And yet. I am in Europe for four months. The kids are grown and I'm supposed to learn who to be without them, this is my only job here (apart from my job). I spent the first three weeks hobbled with loneliness but I walked. I walked listening to podcasts through my headphones because it felt like having friends. Every morning I woke up with that awful lurching in my stomach that meant no one needed anything from me here or even cared if I got out of bed, and also meant I'd have to make all the choices for myself.

But then I taught myself how to be myself. Inch by inch. I went to dinner at a pasta restaurant alone and I thought I'd order a salad, but then I remembered my dinner isn't performative so I got the pasta carbonara with a glass of red wine, okay two glasses. I took the train into Rome over and over, trying out being alone but with podcasts loaded on my phone for loneliness emergencies. I met a few people who didn't know I couldn't make decisions, and I found myself hoping they'd tell me what to do with my life. But we were all grown-ups, so they didn't. The lurching in my stomach gave way just a little.

Nick arrived and it was like I learned to drive a car but someone snatched away my keys. We fell back into our thing, we decided things together, and he fine-tuned things until they were the things he wanted. We cooked the food he likes: sausages and rice and greens. I pretended that this was what I wanted because it wasn't necessarily what I didn't want. We ordered tickets to Naples for a visit and, sure, I wanted to go to Florence instead, but Naples was probably good too. We were fine. Until this moment.

Until the train in Tivoli. Then it spills out all over Platform 2 in whispered shouts. I tell him, "For the first time in my whole life, I got four months to pick things out for myself." I tell him, "I want to pick my own seat on the fucking train." I tell him, "You can't come here on this big thing that I'm doing and just run all over me because I think I might be changing, and I want to be someone who can choose for myself."

And because he's an evolved human, he takes a beat. And another beat. And then he understands. Deeply and fully understands in a way that changes us into newer, better versions of the cool cats we once were. He gets that I can't go back to being a woman carrying paper bags of food I don't want to eat. I don't want frowning to be my full-time job. I just want to pick out my seat on the train and order a pizza for supper instead of cooking.

This is all. It's probably enough.

Beauty Will Save Your Life

Luca is a convert immediately to the church of Nick. They meet on our way to Rome to visit the seven basilicas on a Sunday. This is a pilgrimage lots of Italians do on Sundays where they walk almost the entirety of Rome and stop at the seven biggest churches along the way: Saint Lawrence Outside the Walls, Sanctuary of Our Lady of Divine Love, Basilica of the Holy Cross in Jerusalem, Saint John Lateran, Saint Paul's Outside the Walls, Saint Mary Major, and, finally, Saint Peter's Basilica. It's about a twelve-mile walk where you stop and eat and see things. We're joining Luca and Angela plus two of their friends for the day to practise our Italian and get some culture.

I don't know why I'm so surprised by how many churches there are in Rome but I am. Just like I'm constantly surprised that people are so openly religious, even though I arrived to a life-sized nativity scene outside my door in January. Even though I woke up one morning to the sound of sombre drums beating. And when I got dressed to see what was going on, I saw ten versions of the three wise men following a distinguished pair of Mary and Josephs in a long procession down my street. In January. Even though Luca told me, "I am not so religious" in the same mortified tone someone might use to say, "Sometimes I eat children's toes in the night." For me, whenever someone mentions their religion, it feels like they're telling me something intensely private, like a bra size.

We've come along for the food and the walking instead of the churches, but mostly, Nick is just happy to go anywhere in Italy. After two days he's still just so happy to be with me here. We visit the interiors of the churches as well as just looking at the outsides, which I prefer. I don't precisely know what I'm meant to do inside churches, so I walk around with my hands clasped behind my back and my eyebrows doing that thing, like I'm thinking great thoughts. I'm thinking about the Blundstones I'm wearing and wondering if they'll finally be broken in by the end of the day. Twice now I've worn them for more than a few hours and found myself limping with two numb toes on each foot by the end. I can't limp in front of these chic Roman friends of Luca's, two women called Georgia and Elena, with perfect skin and scarves and health and intricate harem pants made of linen. We don't do it right, Nick and I, especially inside churches. At one church Nick points out the marble busts of former cardinals and popes from the past five hundred years, and they were uniformly detestable, like gargoyles with sneers and bulbous noses and fleshy ears and sagging eyes. I say to Nick, "You'd think they would ask the sculptor to give them a little nip and tuck around the eyes at least," and he smiles but doesn't laugh. We already learned our lesson at the last church when he talked too much about Jesus's perfect abs and no one was happy, especially not the *carabinieri* version of police guarding the entrance.

All the interiors of the churches look the same to me. All equally dark and sleepy with either ornate floors or detailed stained windows or frescoes on the ceilings or all three. People with rosaries sit quietly in pews, their heads bowed in piety. The altar of each church is dramatic, but the pews are simple, hard planks of wood because that's the way I guess it works in churches. I can't help being cynical about all the wealth dripping from the walls of these churches and all the people who are dying of starvation outside these walls. It's a regular thought that boring people probably have, but it sure feels true and horrible standing on marble floors in front of twenty-foot mahogany doors or whatever.

I haven't considered my relationship with religion for a long time. Nick is typically comfortable with Jesus and refers to him as a *good guy*, like they used to play volleyball together in high school. I went to Catholic school until grade eight, first St. Basil's and then St. Mary's in my hometown of Owen Sound. We had religion class and First Communion where we were given little golden books to write about our family tree. This was the age where I found out the man who I thought was my father was never my father at all. This made for a whole lot of confusion in my little golden book with the family tree. I was told by my mom to just keep the right side of my family tree, where there was supposed to be a father, blank, but I wasn't sure what to do about my last name. Grant maybe? This was the man who turned out to be a father to my two little brothers and not me, my mom explained while she was curling my bangs in our washroom one morning, but it was the name I used at school. The only name I knew. I wasn't sure if it belonged to me anymore since he wasn't my father anymore. He was only the guy who picked up my brothers for one weekend a month and took them out for fried chicken and didn't wash their clothes the way my mom liked. What about McGuire? I was told this was the name on my birth certificate, my mother's maiden name and also mine. She didn't like me to use this on account of it being a shameful thing to have a bastard daughter in the seventies. Rouse? The name of my "new" father who was my original father who didn't want me. This was the one thing everyone knew for sure. My mom telling me, "He doesn't want to have a daughter, hon. Sorry." In the voice a person used to say, "No, you can't have another slice of birthday cake. Sorry." After a bunch of crossing out, I went with Grant, and my teacher did that tongue-clucking sad sound but didn't correct me.

I also found out that year that our priest, Father Thompson, didn't want to baptize me because of the bastard thing. He did it under duress, apparently, but he didn't want to. My mom talked about this to one of my aunts when I was hiding under the dinner table as they played cards. I never forgave him. I didn't care about being baptized but it seemed like such a mean thing to do to a little baby. That baby who was me never hurt anyone. She wouldn't hurt anyone for many years to come. After that, when I had to go to confession once a month and got Father Thompson, I lied to him every time. I told him I did things I didn't do, two every time, like fighting or stealing, and then made my third confession that I lied so God wouldn't be mad at me. After a few more years, I stopped thinking about God at all. Father Thompson too. My father has been harder, but I'll get there.

The next time I really thought about God was when my nana was dying. She got sick two weeks after I left my husband when my boys were so little. Just nine, seven, three and two. She was a young grandmother but she was always sick and had been sick for years. Before it wasn't the real kind of sick. It was more the kind you get when you've been a bit under the weather for a few days and then your bed sheets feel grimy with your body heat. Nana wasn't much for healing ever; she loved being sick. Sometimes I imagined her as a little girl, and her mother, who was called Rita and apparently not a loving woman, might have spoiled her a bit when she was sick. Might let her lie in bed with a cold wet face cloth on her forehead. Might make her some soup or read her a book or smooth back her hair. I don't know if this was true, but I do know Nana never felt more loved than when she was ill. She was living with my Aunt Rose by then, merrily ordering moisturizers and viscose-blend pant sets from the Home Shopping Channel until a nurse would come once a day to give her a bath. Every few months or so we'd all get a phone call from my Aunt Rose or her husband, Uncle Dexter, saying, "You should come. It's time."

It was never time until it was.

It was October. I had left my husband with money Nana had given me in August for first and last month's rent. I didn't want to ask her for it, so my Aunt Rose asked her for me. She said yes right away. Said with satisfaction when she gave it to me, "If it's the last thing I do I'm going to get you away from that man," then wrote a cheque and we went to the mall for an Orange Julius. A few months later I got The Call. Straightforward, my Uncle Dexter saying, "You should probably come, hon. Everyone is coming." I drove down to Etobicoke without being worried and figured I'd just make a day of it. Do some shopping, watch a movie with Nana. Maybe get each one of us those chicken pot pies from Swiss Chalet she loved so much. I was never mad about being called for a false alarm and especially not now. Especially when I had a good excuse to escape the unpacked boxes and the loneliness and the kitchen cupboards I suspected would never be full again.

She was nearly ready to die by the time I got there. Her body bloated and the wrong colour. Her new blonde wig gone from her head so any person at all could walk in and see her tender scalp and the age spots and the freckles and the rings so tight on her fingers they'd have to be cut off for sure. I sat by her bed for a few hours wanting to leave. Desperate to leave. My ears ringing with the effort it took to stay put. She mumbled in her sleep and shifted, her standing fan blowing on her face as she slept near death, just as it always had.

I thought about all the times I slept beside her in a different bed, the one from the house where I grew up. All the times we'd go for a nap in the heavy heat of summer when I was a little girl and again when I was mostly grown. Her bedroom dark but for her bedside light, a stack of books leaning against the dusty white lamp with heavy fringe on the shade. An ashtray, a half-eaten box of Laura Secord chocolates with the orange creams left for me. Not sleeping but resting, we called it, with her reading a thick romance novel and me lying there with my eyes closed. Her stroking my hair with one hand between flipping pages — when I was five and again when I was fifteen and again when I was pregnant for the first time. When we baked raisin bread for Christmas and took long nap breaks during the afternoon, me pregnant with the person who would be Callum. Climbing under her duvet with the house smelling of nutmeg and cinnamon and a touch of pumpkin and the snow outside.

I sat there and watched her sleep for three hours the day she died. She was never Nana at all then, mumbling violently, sometimes afraid. She didn't want to die ever. She just wanted us to be afraid she'd die so she could watch her own funeral play out at her bedside. But here she was, not awake or aware enough to know we were all here. And we, all wanting her to be here and stay here.

After a while I had to leave to get my boys and leaned over and said, "Nana, I have to go." And just like that, there she was, awake. Herself. Clear-eyed in her puffy face. "Are you on your way, honey?" No one else was in the room with us for that one minute. The Halloween orange sun was setting outside through her half-open bedroom blinds. It was late afternoon, around five or so, and the rest of my family was downstairs starting to think about what to do about dinner. Probably potato salad and a rotisserie chicken or something. I wouldn't be there then. I wouldn't be there when she died later that night in her sleep. I felt this in that long, slow moment. I said, "Um, yeah. Nana? You know I love you right?" Because what else was there. She smiled at me, fully in my face with her whole face. Our shared history a palpable thing hanging between us, "Oh, I sure do love you, honey." Then she retreated back to the place where she was going.

That was the only time I felt God.

The walk around Rome ends in a revelation. The food, so much food. We stop along the way for another latte and a *cornetto* and a glass of wine and, finally, some Indian food near Termini, where we all order different meals and share like we're a family. Angela orders me a chai with honey and coconut milk whether I want it or not. The churches are fine but it's places like Trevi Fountain, a place I never thought I'd see in the whole of my life, that get to me. Get to me in a way that, when I stand there, all the buzzing in my ears from trying to assimilate goes quiet. The bright-blue water smells like no other water, the fountain is loud over the small crowd. Angela says, "You are lucky it is January. Normally, you can get nowhere near the fountain." I see it then. I see the impossible beauty of it. I'm dazzled completely. More than the basilicas or the Pantheon or the Colosseum, this is the Rome I signed up for. I think of Tim worrying I wouldn't learn to see Rome as more than just a pile of rocks. He was right and he was wrong. This right here. This fountain built in 19 BC during the reign of Augustus Caesar. This speaks to me. It's my cinematic moment and I'm standing in it. I'm touching the marble curving around the pool of water and seeing the coins thrown for luck, just like I said I would. I said I'd do this thing, and I'm doing it and it feels so exactly right. I see I'm lucky, and I start to cry behind my sunglasses in a way that everyone knows I'm crying. Nick shifts to stand closer so no one will see but they do. Georgia, the shorter of the two new friends, with clear skin and a short pixie cut and a heart-shaped face, nods and says to me, "You are correct to cry. Beauty, it will save your life."

And Now I Know for Sure

Nick flew home on a Tuesday. We came back from spending a weekend visiting Naples and Sorrento and not being romantic at all. He tried, he always tries, but there's this blockage in me that he sometimes can't chip away at, no matter what he might have in his tool box. I can't either. It started out well. We took the high-speed train to Naples, and Nick was flabbergasted at the technology. We brought coffees and *cornetti* for the short ride. "An hour and a half, can you believe that?" Nick kept taking videos of the passing landscape and updating me on the speed of the train posted at the front of the car: "295, 300, 350..." When we arrived in this mean, grubby port city it was raining and we immediately got lost and I couldn't forgive him.

I don't know what it is in me. I wanted to never forgive him, even if this wasn't his fault. He wanted pizza in Naples, this was why we came, and I resented him, oh my God, did I resent him. I resented giving up a single day of my stay here for him, and I refused to think about the fact that I had no other plans at all. It wasn't his fault that we got lost, he just asked someone when we left the train station who wasn't interested in helping us. After an hour or so of wandering, through the fog of my stubborn irritation with him, my heart melted a little, seeing him desperately struggling to figure out where we should be going. Trying to find me an umbrella, trying to find us pizza, trying to salvage a day he didn't ruin in the first place. My face was closed to him entirely and I couldn't have explained why. I still can't. When we finally found our way, picking through the unhappy busy streets of Naples, where it felt as though every person we saw was trying to rob us, I refused to eat. This was something I said I'd never do but there I was, arms and legs crossed so tight that the waiters looked at Nick with real sympathy. *Poor guy,* they thought, *eating his pizza with a lump in his throat.*

There's this joke with our friends about how Nick is lucky if he gets to come in fifth place, and I'm proud of this. I've always been proud of it. I'm proud that I will not become a mom who chooses her new man over her kids. I'm proud they know they're the loves of my life.

For Nick, it's not like this. For Nick, I'm first. He told me this once in the middle of some ridiculous fight over the phone when he was in Toronto and I was in Owen Sound, and one or both of us had been drinking too much. He said to me in this desperate voice, "You are above everyone to me. You're top of the heap. I love you more than anyone." I heard how he wanted me to say it to him, and I could have but I wouldn't. I'm attached to my version of us, where he is wrong for me in all the ways.

I relented at that dingy pizzeria in Naples. Apologized to him. "I'm sorry. I know it's not your fault it's raining. I'm just so disappointed by Naples." "It's shitty," he agreed on an exhale that was pure relief. We'd been warned by other Italians that it wouldn't be a friendly spot, but Nick wanted a pizza in Naples and so we came. "Why don't we go to Sorrento and skip Naples?"

And so we did but we couldn't get the romance back. Since he'd arrived in Italy, I was cheap with my affection when I thought about it and easy with it when I didn't. Most nights I fell asleep with my back to him and woke up wound around him tight as a ribbon on a Christmas present. In Sorrento, we wandered around the abandoned seaside town. The Italians there were nice, friendly. Sharing advice on where to eat dinner when we stopped for an espresso and a snack to get out of the rain. It was a small bakery close to the train station run by two sisters, both about sixty or so, in white aprons over their black slacks and t-shirts. They told us to try out Acqu'e Sale, a seafood place at the water's edge at the bottom of the cliff. It was one of those white-and-blue stucco buildings that suited Sorrento, a chic little jewel of a town high above the sea. We climbed down about three hundred stairs to find delicious pizza in a restaurant where a fire roared in the big pot-bellied wood oven and the wine was good and the waiters were solicitous. Nick looked so good, his salt-and-pepper hair a little wet and his eyes with that mischievous glint he doesn't know he gets sometimes. We climbed back up the stairs, back to the Airbnb I'd rented on the cheap since it was off season. I climbed into bed to read a book; he stayed up listening to music and scrolling through weather details on his phone. We barely kissed goodnight, and I didn't know why. I still can't understand why. *This*, I thought, *this is the end*.

We spent our last night in the little cave together in Tivoli, eating charcuterie bits and pieces with leftover pizza. Some prosciutto and marinated artichokes and a wedge of sharp cheese. The good olives and some dark greens sautéed in some sort of garlic and lemon that Nick had learned to make from his own nonna, rapini I think it was called. We drank wine and beer. He played the guitar, and I sang "Mambo Italiano" and some other cliché Italian music we know. We arranged for Fabrizio to take him to the airport the next morning to simplify everything. And we had relaxed, easy sex when we went to bed. The kind of sex that makes you languid and sleepy and loved, and I thought, *If this is the end it's a good one.*

The next morning Nick had to leave by seven. *Okay*, I thought. *Okay.* I walked him to the curb. His face a bit drawn but always with that look like he wanted to smile. He really just wanted to smile, that was all there is for Nick. That's always his end goal. I hugged him. Hard. And then I wouldn't stop hugging him. I couldn't stop. I stood there with him in the circle of my arms, my hands on the flat part between his shoulder blades. I choked on my sobs while Fabrizio idled his airport limo close by. Nick said, "I know. I know." His hands trying to steady me on the cobblestones as I clutched him, climbed him, clawed at him. He tried to steady me because he understood I didn't want to let him go.

And I guess this is the true thing about him. I didn't know, but he did. He knew I loved him even when I didn't want to. When he was too complicated for me and too old. God, how many more times can I say he was too old, too placid, too sweet. But as some song probably goes, I couldn't help loving him. And all of a sudden I didn't want to help it. He left, he had to. He left me standing there on the cobblestones sobbing while little Fiats and scooters sped past me, whipping up the air at our sides so we both shifted. I stood there watching him leave and just wanted to say over and over, "I'm sorry."

The cave is imprinted by Nick. His shampoo and soap in the shower. His guitar pick in the little bowl on the kitchen table. The tray set up for me to work on my laptop in bed so I can be, like he said, "well and truly ensconced" while I write. The fridge full of leftovers carefully wrapped up for me, eggs and cheese and bread and greens. The coffee maker he bought on the kitchen counter, so we could have a fresh pot in the morning while dabbling in the Canadian crosswords he stockpiled to bring me. My laundry bag is full of fresh, dry-cleaned clothes from the laundromat he found for me. All my recycling was taken away by him, and the trash system I could never figure out was negotiated and dealt with accordingly. He was everywhere except here.

This is my darkest day. The day I don't think I can stay. Not just because Nick left but because of how much I've squandered by refusing to love him when I should. By listening to people like Gina, my oldest friend, the one who I went to Switzerland with as an au pair twenty-five years ago, who told me, "Honestly, I'm so sick of Nick's storyline. Girl, you are going to Europe and you are going to fuck so many hot guys and you won't even remember Nick. Guys will be all over you, especially now." I told her I wasn't going to Europe to meet men and she answered, "Okay, so then why bother?" Maybe I thought she was right. Maybe I thought I deserved someone better than Nick. Maybe I was settling like she said.

Now he's going back to Canada, and I won't see him for three months. And I'm drowning. I go for a walk through fields of olive trees where there are still remnants of the ancient Roman road. I pass the town square we liked best; the stairs where I'd sit to write in my journals and drink tea while he painted when the light was right in the late-afternoon sun. This square is beside a school and a tiny chapel. School children would come out when the bell rang to watch him paint and call for their mothers to watch too. I pass Rocca Pia, an old battlement in Tivoli where we went on a tour in Italian that neither of us understood, and afterwards, ate veal sandwiches with beer in the drizzling rain, sitting on the same side of the table and kissing like we were new. We felt so new.

I ask to take the day off from work. I climb back into bed and watch episodes of *Grace and Frankie* on Netflix for so long I have to keep turning myself like a rotisserie chicken to avoid bed sores. Luca and Angela invite me for dinner and I say no. Renato invites me for dinner and I say no.

I don't want anyone but Nick. At last.

She Knows You're a Mama

Ravioli is a passion of Luca's, and I guess it's a passion of mine too. Before he finally introduced me to the very best ravioli, the kind where he clasps his hands together in a back-and-forth prayer, he talked about the very best ravioli for two weeks — the ravioli from Il Braciere in San Polo. He'd talk about this while he was eating subpar ravioli somewhere else. He talked about it when he cooked his other favourite dish, called pasta carbonara, which he said he made for Angela, but Nick and I knew it might have mostly been for him. He talked about it when we walked around Rome, where a person could be forgiven for assuming there was probably some pretty delicious ravioli to be had. I didn't tell Luca that my favourite ravioli before coming to Italy was the Chef Boyardee kind.

This seems like I'm kidding but I'm definitely not. When I was in high school, my boyfriend Mark would bring cans of mini ravioli to my house on nights when my mom was out. We'd cook it on the stove and eat it with a short stack of buttered white bread while watching rented movies. If I was babysitting for any of my aunts, my only form of payment was cans of mini ravioli, *not* Beefaroni. As an adult I stopped eating this kind of ravioli, it wasn't worth the calories, especially since I only wanted to eat it with buttered white bread. I didn't share Luca's passion for ravioli at first. I didn't really have a great passion for pasta at all. It wasn't why I decided to go to Italy. I like pizza a lot and cheese and pasta and different sauces. But in my first weeks, I will tell you, the lack of variety got to me. More pizza, more spaghetti, more fettuccine, yes, I was getting it. Until Il Braciere.

It's a Friday when Luca and I finally decide to try hiking to San Polo dei Cavalieri. I meet him at 8:00 a.m. and he brings walking sticks and water and cookies for us both. I bring my cell phone, just for me. The trek is about twenty-five miles total and the village of San Polo dei Cavalieri is at the top of a curlicue road that looks like a swirl of soft-serve ice cream coming out from the green trees below. Luca has never hiked this way, but I trust him. Mostly because he looks worried, like in his brain he could already see the headline: *Canadian Mother of Four Dies after Being Led into the Woods by Swarthy Italian*. He'll make sure we arrive safely, if only to avoid an international disaster for Tivoli, since he's really hoping to help the tourism market take off.

The hike takes us back up the same mountain where I first met him and Francesco. That was a month ago or a year ago or a decade ago. It feels more than anything like another life. Since then, I've gone on a few of the guided tours with Francesco to help him with his English, which is good, but he never thinks it's good enough. Like everyone trying to learn a new language, he leans heavily on the same phrases over and over again. "This cow is not dangerous." "There might be wolves but they are not dangerous." "The many spiders and small snakes slithering through the tall grass are not dangerous." I thought it was funny until we were out for a hike with some young American girls and they snickered. I hated them plus me.

Luca and I have an easy time hiking up the mountain at first. We don't talk much because of the language thing but also the morning thing. It's difficult enough for me to string more than "*si*," "*grazie*" and "*prego*" together when I'm fully awake, but in the morning, even the thought of making these attempts has me feeling mutinous. I suspect it's the same for Luca, so he forges on ahead of me thinking his thoughts in natural Italian without being forced to translate. At one point he asks me how to say "mud" because we're slipping in mud on the way up a particularly steep hill. I say, "It's *mud*." And he says, "Made?" And I say, "Mud," and this goes on like a routine that isn't so funny. He tells me it's called *fango* in Italian, so this is the word we use.

We don't start to get into the groove of our hike until the sun is fully up in the sky, so hot and bright we both have to shed a sweatshirt layer. We stop and drink water then open the gate that will have us crossing into the Way of the Wolf, the first time for us both. The path is especially gravelly here and on the side of a cliff. To the right is a stunning view of the valley dotted with groups of ten or twelve houses that look close enough together to string a clothesline for laundry between them but are likely miles apart. The view might be lovely but the path is narrow, so narrow, my feet are at an angle in my boots while I walk. There's no fence to protect me from falling, and on the other side of me are cows with horns and bells around their necks that tinkle every time they eat grass, which is always. I've heard rumours from Francesco that these cows are not dangerous but they are large and unblinking and everywhere. Luca tells me not to worry — until we see a bull.

At that point he reaches back to grab my arm, tells me to keep my head down and walk faster and faster.

Eventually the path takes a left turn and we're in the cool forest. We're also ready to talk and we manage. We talk about our childhoods, both of us grew up with brothers. Luca is the oldest and has twin brothers while I am the oldest and have brothers who might as well be twins because they like to be best friends without me. He tells me about how he lived with his parents until he married Angela, and he lets me dig really deep into that topic. I ask him why so many Italian men live with their parents for so long and he says, "It is different here in Italy. We stay with our parents to save money. It would be insulting to move out for no good reason. When you get married, this is the time to move. But not before." I wonder how that would work with dating and sex and being a grown-up and he says, "You always find ways. Your mother has to sleep sometime, you know?" This makes me think of my sons and the times when they might have thought I was sleeping in my room but they were dead wrong. The things I heard that I never wanted to hear and could never unhear.

I change the subject to extramarital affairs. I've always heard that European men, Italians specifically, are very comfortable with extramarital affairs. When I ask Luca about this, he gets this wry smile on his face. "For me, I would not do this. But it is understood with some men that if you are discreet and you do not get emotional about this other woman, it is fine." He points out, "I think it is this way in America and Canada too for many people." I think he's probably right but I wish he was wrong.

We hike for another hour or so, sharing our stories in English and Italian until we come to a stucco house with vines all over (inside and out) and a clawfoot tub in the yard.

Several broken-down cars litter the lawn; some tarps, tacked poorly to one window frame, flap in the breeze. We're about to walk by when a dog comes wandering out, a Bernese mountain dog with her little puppy bounding out after her. This puppy is terrified of us. When I try to approach, he cries and cries but continues to follow his mother, who is now leading Luca on the path like it's her calling. That dog never looks back at her baby, not once.

I imagine this little pup lost and alone. Unable to find food, hit by a car, falling off a cliff. We reach the end of the trail and have to walk on the road for the rest of the climb to San Polo. I think the dogs will leave us there as we climb along the road but they don't.

The mother walks on ahead and easily steps out of the way of small Italian cars whipping blindly around those curlicue corners. I don't think the puppy has ever seen a car. Cars keep coming and I keep wincing. Keep begging the puppy to go back and then go to the side and then just stay with me or let me carry him. I say it like he understands. Luca calls back, "Jennifer, you have to just come, so he will follow. Hurry up." The climb is hard, 2,100 feet above sea level, but I take it at a run. The puppy runs after me, and we're together safe on the side of the road. Luca and the mother are waiting for us at the top, her head turned away from us looking forward to her destiny, I guess. Before I can stop myself, I scream at her, "What's wrong with you? How could you leave your baby?" She ignores me, head high, dignified. But Luca says gently, "She leaves her baby with you. She knows you are a mama. She knows you keep him safe so she can do her job."

We walk along in silence after this, Luca's back to me and the dog's back to me too. The little puppy has calmed down and walks beside me, glancing up at me the same way my kids used to when they thought I was about to cry. When I was having a bad day and they didn't want to ask and they didn't know what to do with me. Nervous, cautious, waiting.

I don't cry. Instead, I think this dog shouldn't trust me with her baby. I don't know what I'm doing. This puppy could get hurt and it'll be my fault. It is my fault. It's always my fault. I think of my babies, and I think, *It's my fault.* And I don't know what I'm blaming myself for — Jack's teeth grinding in his sleep or Callum's stress that made him sick to his stomach or Ben's constant self-doubt or Nathan's anxiety. I don't know if it's their bruises or their hurts or their beds that didn't have the right sheets (sometimes no sheets at all). I don't know what I think is my fault — but then, all of a sudden, I stop for just a minute. I stop because a wild dog saw something in me that she trusted. That she could sense I was a mother and that I might even be a good one sometimes. That I do my best. For just a minute, I know I did a good job. I think I did a good job. I got the puppy to safety. I got us all to safety. I did the best I could.

The dogs finally leave us in town, and Il Braciere is closed. But we find a different restaurant where the ravioli is a religious experience. I eat and eat ravioli. I drink and drink white wine. I feel better, even though I didn't really know I was feeling bad before. The walk home is faster, quieter. We're tired from eating so much food and maybe a little drunk. We pass the house again but it's really abandoned this time. There are no dogs to guide us. I guess they've already shown us the way.

Peanut Butter and Onion Sandwich

I left my husband, David, when he was at work. I took my four boys in my 1999 Mazda MPV minivan and left our house in a good suburb in Barrie with a big bright kitchen and a family room freshly painted cayenne-pepper red. I left our master bedroom with the walk-in closet and the ensuite bath and the sitting room. I left our formal dining room and our living room and our walkout basement that housed the boys' ride-on toys and also my brother.

When I left my husband, I did it suddenly. I didn't plan anything. I tried planning to leave in the months after Nathan was born. I tucked money away from my waitressing job at a local pub when I could. It was perfectly awful. Every day I had to pretend all the time. I had to pretend I wanted to stay with him. Sometimes when he was very kind or we were just regular people watching a movie on the couch, I had to pretend I wanted to leave him. I had to pretend I didn't have a small roll of bills tied up with one of my hair elastics in my secondary makeup bag under the sink in our ensuite bath. It turns out I didn't have to pretend all that time; it was wasted acting. He found the money one day while I was at work. And then my hundreds of dollars for the first and last month's rent was for him only. He bought a new DVD player and DVDs to go in that player and a PlayStation and, I guess, some beer.

When I did leave him, I didn't know it was coming until I sat at a stop sign after dropping him at work. I was supposed to turn right to go home. I just couldn't do it. I sat there with that *click-click, click-click* of my turn signal until nine-year-old Callum said from his third-row seat, "Mom!" So I left my husband just like that.

We weren't dressed to leave that day. We had five diapers and three-year-old Jack was wearing Superman pyjamas with the attached cape and his second-best sandals. We didn't have sunscreen, which would be a problem for seven-year-old Ben in August because he burned so easily. Nathan was only two and just sitting there in his car seat being two. I had around $150 in my bank account so I got some gas and some McDonald's. I let Callum sit beside me in the front seat so he could be the deejay as we drove. This was when I went home to Owen Sound. This was when I went to my aunt's house and stayed the night. This was when we called my nana and she said, "Whatever it takes for you to leave him, I'll give it to you." She meant first and last month's rent only, but it felt like more. It felt like applause for something I still wasn't sure I was deciding to do.

It took only one month to do all my layers of leaving. First, I left my husband. This part was hard because I still really wanted to be the family who stayed together and lived in a big house and had dinner parties on the weekends, where the kids would run around together in the yard and play with sparklers as the sun went down. *We both want this*, I thought. But if we were a sandwich, we'd be a peanut butter and onion sandwich and no one wants to eat that, not even us.

I didn't like David and he didn't like me, but he didn't want me to be the one to leave him and take his children. In the beginning, he pretended the two older boys were also his children like we'd always done; like we should never have done.

When I told Callum and Ben that we were moving to Owen Sound where there are trees and they could go to a nice small school with new friends and have a new house but no dad, they pretended to be sad, but not really. They weren't really sad at all, just sat on my bed (that was just *my* bed all of a sudden) while I explained. Ben looked at Callum for how to react and Callum looked at me and I looked at the floor. Callum said, "Well, that's okay then." He was already tired of pretending this man was his dad and for him the world looked wide open all of a sudden. Ben was ready to give him up too if that was the way the wind was blowing and if I promised he could have Kernels dill pickle popcorn the next time we went to the mall. "A whole one just for myself," he said. This was the deal we made.

David's affections changed just as easily. In a month, he had a new job and a new woman and an old family that was easy to forget, so easy.

Then there was the next layer, called leaving my house in Barrie. It was harder. Our house was rented but didn't look rented. If you asked the neighbours, they never would have guessed. It was an executive home in an executive neighbourhood with three parks we could walk to. My brother rented the basement and this was how we afforded to live there. He didn't like that I was moving but he forgave me once he found a new place to live.

Also there was David's mom. She was hard. She loved all the boys for real. She'd make Ben lunches of toasted hot dog buns with his own personal bottle of ketchup when he ordered, "Hot dog, hold the wiener please." She cried when she found out, and she cries sometimes still, from what Jack and Nathan tell me. I loved her. I love her.

My mom. She was the hardest. She lived in Barrie too, just a few blocks from my house. She was away on holiday when I left and felt cheated by my leaving. She didn't like David. She wanted me to stay so we could go to Walmart together on Saturdays to pick up a few things or go try on clothes at the Gap or eat mall Chinese food with Jack and Nathan while Callum and Ben were at school. She wanted family dinners on Wednesdays, where we cook the food and clean the kitchen, and she is happy, happy, happy. I told her that, when I leave, this won't change but this lie was embarrassing for us both.

I went back to Barrie to pack us up and there you have it. I was away. When I drove back to Owen Sound at the end of August, one month after my big decision, my kids were signed up for school and we had a nice house. I had a good, reliable vehicle and a bit of savings in my account. I listened to one song over and over, a song about a person who is always making me ill.

That was David. He was making me ill.

We were married for only five years, but David made me ill. He made me afraid. He made me forget that I could be good and kind and funny and loved. He told me that people would hate me if they knew me as well as he knew me. He told me this often and I believed him every time. He laughed the hardest if I fell and hurt myself. He talked about our sex life at dinner parties. He told the other husbands he'd never put up with a woman who turned down sex when he wanted it while I was serving burned lasagna with my burning face.

He told Callum and Ben they weren't good enough. He disciplined them with passion and loved them with reserve. If they didn't eat their dinner, he'd keep them at the table for hours and hours while I was at work. I always worked. I went back to work when Jack and Nathan were each six weeks old and my breasts still leaked. No one wanted me there, least of all me. I'd leave my boys with lipstick kisses on their foreheads and come home to see Callum had cried himself to sleep, still wearing his jeans and t-shirt and baseball cap. His breathing would still have that hitch in it like when he cried, it was like his body still knew he was sad. My lipstick kiss would still be there but it didn't matter anymore. I had left him. The deed was done.

David loved his own sons like furniture he was still putting together and wasn't quite sure he'd keep. He threw Jack into his father's swimming pool to teach him to swim when I wasn't there to stop it. Somehow, I was never there to stop it. He turned the baby monitor off so I couldn't hear Nathan crying for me, but I'll tell you something, I always knew when my baby cried for me. I didn't know a lot but this I knew.

He wanted them to love him like they loved me, but here was the truth about my boys and me then, we didn't love anyone like we loved each other.

The Arrogance of Pigeons

I have a problem with pigeons. Every single bird frightens me, but pigeons are the worst, followed closely by seagulls. The first time I knew I was afraid of birds, I was about five years old in the backyard of Chandi Fernando, one of my best friends on the street when my mom and my brothers and I lived with my grandparents. Chandi lived on the river side of the street, her yard sloping down to the nut-brown Pottawatomi as it flowed past. We were playing on her swing set on a sunny summer morning when we saw a fluffy duckling and were instantly enchanted. I've tried to bring that feeling back, the easy love I felt for a little duckling, but I can't. We were watching it waddle through her yard when two seagulls swooped down from the sky and lifted it into the air. They tossed it back and forth between them and ripped it to shreds. First, they snapped its neck, then when parts of it fell to the ground, they fought each other to eat what was left over. That was the end for me and birds right there.

It's no easy thing being afraid of birds. They're everywhere and everyone loves them. No fewer than a dozen people have tried to convert me to becoming a bird lover or, at least, a bird accepter. One of Nick's neighbours has a side porch dotted with bird feeders and she tried to persuade me to come out and feed the swooping hummingbirds no less than five times. "They're amazing creatures," she told me, but I never heard anything beyond the loud drone of their eternally flapping wings. Another teenager (who worked at a beloved local toy store) brought her pet chicken for one of those Easter petting zoo affairs when my boys were little. The owner of the store knew I was afraid of birds, everyone in town knew, but this girl followed me around the store with that chicken softly clucking in her arms. Needing her pet to cure me. I have friends who go to the beach and argue that their children should be allowed to feed the seagulls as part of some rite of passage. Friends who laugh and say, "They're only birds!" when I explain I can't eat alfresco. Friends who explain that birds won't kill me, like this is my concern. Like I'm convinced that birds will kill me. I know better. They won't kill me but they can't be trusted. They aren't predictable.

There's no one in my life who isn't aware of my ornithophobia, everyone's been touched by it. My sons have grown up with it. Callum always screaming, "Mom! God!" when I flinch away from a chickadee on the sidewalk or cross the street if a seagull is perched on a trash can nearby. It seems like a funny quirk, but go ahead and think about how a person can avoid birds and the answer is there's no way at all.

When the boys were younger, we went to Sauble Beach as often as our broken-down minivan could handle taking the twenty-minute trip. We'd get ourselves set up with books and blue collapsible folding chairs, plus a blanket and two pillows for anyone who needed to stretch out. The boys always ran into the water leaving a trail of t-shirts and flip flops in their wake and I settled in with my journal for an afternoon of writing in the sun. Then some family would set up on the sand beside us with bags of salt-and-vinegar chips that they'd leave open on their own blanket. *No umbrella, no cooler, no concern for us* — this is what I thought every time. The seagulls would flock but the family would be long gone, tossing the football around in the water, and we'd have to go home. Or seagulls would inexplicably fall dead beside me out of the sky, and we'd have to go home. Or I'd accidentally disturb a nest of terns and the mother would dive-bomb my head as I'd crab-scuttle back to the shore screaming and gulping water as I went, and we'd have to go home. Whenever someone thinks my bird fear is funny, my kids tell this story and others. About all the times they had to leave a place or hide or worse, shield me from a Canadian goose or a seagull or a hummingbird. But pigeons are the worst.

In Italy pigeons are everywhere. Pigeons roosting in the cracks between the stones of houses, their cooing louder than my headphones no matter how high I crank the volume. They have two states of being, lying in wait for me to pass or manically flying towards me en masse. There's no middle ground. At the top of my street in Tivoli there's a courtyard where people gather to watch the sunset, maybe enjoy a slice of pizza from Ugo's with sausage and mushrooms and a boiled egg sliced delicately on top, for around three euros. The courtyard has a little fountain where locals gather to fill water jugs and disposable plastic bottles, the water as pure and cold as anything.

Men sit outside a small fruit market talking and smoking for hours at a time. They feed pigeons no matter what, no matter the time of day and no matter who is walking by.

Twice now I've been climbing the hill with my head down and earphones in, a friendly English-speaking podcast in my ear, when I've found myself surrounded by pigeons.

Both times I've jerked my body back and screamed my lungs out, indiscriminate wings surrounding me as they fly off with crumbs of food gifted to them by humans. One man said to me in Italian, "It's just a pigeon." (I'm so sick of hearing this in every language.) As though I might not know which animal was flying at me. As though no one has ever been afraid of a pigeon. Another said, "*Tranquile, senora,*" which means "calm down," and no one in any language has ever calmed down when someone said calm down. No one ever.

The frequency of pigeons has become a real problem for me in Italy. I can't figure them out, can't anticipate their movements. When walking down charming cobbled streets with sidewalk cafés, I keep a weather eye out for pigeons under tables hoping for scraps of food. When I see them, I track them for a bit. I watch them walk slowly to the left, I move to the right, and that's when they too decide to pivot. I can't bring myself to admit my fear to anyone else. It's information I usually share after I have at least had the chance to be charming or funny or interesting, which I can't pull off in my broken, halting, gesturing Italian. But Luca knows. He's caught me flinching one too many times. He gave me the words in Italian, *Ho paura degli uccelli* — "I'm afraid of birds."

Other than with Luca, I'm on my own with my pigeon fear and I have to pay close attention to where I walk, crossing streets to avoid a cooing cluster and ducking low when they swoop down from their nests or whatever. They sometimes fly into the train station and approach my feet as I try to buy a ticket from the machine with its constant lecture in English, "Beware of pickpockets."

Eating outside at home has been out of the question for years now. Any kind of snack that gives off a scent that birds could pick up, like french fries or hot dogs or really anything save a bottle of water, is off limits. In Canada, Nick found a few patios with those wires overhead to keep the seagulls away but, the truth is, I never really trust them. Birds can swoop in from left and right not just from above; this is common knowledge.

It's one thing to startle and scream when you're with other people but quite another when you spend most of your days exploring on your own. I don't like the looks I get from people, like the woman beside me on the platform waiting to catch the train into Rome. A pigeon snuck silently under my bench while I looked the other way and it startled me when it flew off. I jerked a bit and dropped my phone, scrambling among the old cigarette butts and gum ground into the pavement to retrieve it. Her look of disgust stayed firmly in place all the way to Rome.

I am constantly vigilant and start to avoid some of the more popular public places, like the Spanish Steps, where too many people eat gelato, and Campo de' Fiori, a hotbed of streetside cafés. When movies are filmed in Europe, there are no pigeons walking through the streets and I've wondered about this many times. It feels like an airbrushing of sorts, a pointless lie.

There is one exception to walking the streets of Rome without fear, and this is at nighttime. Luca invited me along to dinner with some of his friends one night, at a little side-street restaurant close to Campo de' Fiori, and it was an experience. Rome at night. In January there are very few tourists and the city feels like it's glowing just for me. Oh, the freedom, the confidence of a nighttime walk through the city without fear of a pigeon crossing. Just walking freely through the streets of Rome at midnight alongside six Italian men who had let me into their circle, including Luca's younger brother

Marco, a big softie whom I liked immediately. An emotional man, he wept several times within the first hour of our meeting. Once about how much he loved his little boys and then about the movie *Bohemian Rhapsody* that he'd just seen. The four other men, all impeccably dressed in dark pants and dark shirts and soft scarves worn elegantly under dark coats, didn't speak much English, but still took great pleasure in seeing me taste food all night. "*Provare, provare,*" they said again and again as I tasted one man's lasagna and another's pasta carbonara and some prosciutto and some eggplant parmigiana and tiramisu and coffee and the little cups of liqueur we sipped with our biscotti.

After our long dinner, perhaps three hours of eating and talking, we walked over to the Piazza Navona, almost barren of people. We found a little terrace with heaters and blankets and drank a bit more, each of us languid and comfortable with each other in the way of carbohydrate eaters.

We walked back to Luca's car together around one in the morning, my steps were sure and bold and joyful. I didn't have to tell these men about my bird fear, they didn't have to suffer through my panicked grabs at their arms or leaping behind one of them in an effort to escape a pigeon. Instead, we just ate food and tried to talk to each other, but mostly, we ate and drank and lived.

This, I thought, *is what my life would be like without birds.* And the wide-open world of possibility I'd never see to fruition was almost too beautiful for me to bear.

Sophia Loren's Villa

Claudio and I park our bikes side by side and wait for the others to catch up. The sun is shining low and flattering, casting that good late-morning glow on our faces and shoulders only. We are quiet after two hours of getting to know each other in Italian, English and Mandarin (all the languages between our group of seven). We met that morning at a bar for a quick coffee and a chat before heading off for the day to cycle the old Appian Way together. It's just me and a family of four from China, all of whom are polite and speak excellent English but really just want to hang back by themselves. Right away, I saw that they were trying not to be responsible for starting a conversation with me and this is fine. I'd been trying to book this cycling day for the past six weeks (struggling after my credit card was compromised and I lost access to Airbnb). I'm finally here and I just want to be here, really be here. Claudio and Sergio are our guides, the first tall and slender with sort of scholarly long hair and the other short and tanned and moustached. Claudio wears old jeans and a moth-eaten dark-green sweater, in the way of an aristocratic child of means who chooses to wear such things, and a light batik scarf tossed carelessly over one shoulder that never moves throughout our day of cycling, not once. Sergio is in bike shorts, a skin-tight Lycra shirt covered in premium bike logos, goggles and wristbands. And a hat that is neither a baseball cap nor a bucket hat, pulled low. Looking at their two outfits that morning, I wasn't quite sure what sort of bike ride this would turn out to be, leisurely like Claudio or sporty like Sergio. Turns out this is a Claudio sort of day.

We rode away from the edge of the city at first, Claudio nervously watching like a mother duck to make sure we all got through the green light because, as he said, "Romans will just run you down. They don't give a shit." This hasn't been my experience; in my opinion they simply respond well to confidence. If you want to cross the street you must step in front of a speeding car and hope for the best, shoulders squared against insults and injury. We all survived our crossing and made our way past a decrepit, beautiful old farm to Ninfeo di Egeria, where the city suddenly quieted. There were cats, of course there were cats. Everywhere there were cats. Even the place where Julius Caesar was so famously stabbed by his senators became a sanctuary for cats. Not that they need one, cats are sacred here. Tivoli has so many wild dogs that a person has to hang their garbage from a peg on their wall for the sanitation men to come pick it up in the middle of the night, otherwise packs of dogs will rip it to pieces. But people like Sergio carry cans of tuna and other little treats in their backpacks for any cat they might encounter. He told me there was indeed a cat who is very special to him on this trip. One who lives along the ancient roads bordered by villas of famous people like Sophia Loren and who suns himself on the bust of a dead wealthy family.

Our first stop at Ninfeo di Egeria is a stone grotto surrounded by cool green moss and trees. Claudio gives me a little history of the grotto but I am more interested in finding out about him, a local with perfect English. He tells me he works two jobs, cycling tour guide and Latin teacher. He is soft-spoken and polite, apologetic about the inherent clichéd arrogance of so many Roman men. "It's embarrassing that these men walk about so arrogantly because of something other men did thousands of years before they were born. They do nothing to be proud of." He explains that the men of Rome walk about with their shoulders back and their heads high, rude to tourists and spoiled by their mothers until they find a forgiving wife who spoils them further. I say nothing on account of knowing only three or four Romans so far, maybe six now, including Luca's parents.

I met Luca's parents once when we met his friends for dinner in Rome. They were both very gracious and cosmopolitan. His mother is an artist of some renown and speaks excellent French; his father, a Roman historian. Their apartment was beautiful and filled with art and antiques and welcoming in the way where they don't care if you put your feet up. I thought, *I don't blame Luca for staying in this apartment so long. There's a bidet and also a bathtub.* When I told his mother I left my sons behind in Canada she politely tried to hide her shock. Took a sip of her small glass of red wine and looked down at the table and said, "I'm sure this is very nice for you." I pointed out that they already lived on their own and she was too polite to make a big deal out of it, but I saw myself going down in her estimation. "It's a cultural thing," Luca noted.

Leaving my sons behind in Canada is one of those things I tell other mothers about for a whole bunch of different reasons. Because I want them to think I'm cool, because I want them to see that they're going to have to prepare themselves for an eventual empty nest and it's a lot harder than they might realize. Because I want them to envy me. Because I want them to like me. Except I never tell people how awful it was in the beginning and how it kept being awful.

I've been nearly two months away from the boys, and I wake up every morning wrong-footed and panicked. Like I stepped off a curb and am perpetually between tripping and falling. Before I'm fully awake and can slip my free-spirited travel mask on, I just stay in bed with my eyes closed, thinking about the best way to get through my day until I can come back here and go to sleep. I think about how many times the boys have called me in a panic over this and that. This one was running out of money and worried about rent. That one not doing well in school. The other having girlfriend problems. Some of them I can fix but some I can't. The worst problem is that they feed me only little appetizers of their lives over the phone. And I'm hungry, always hungry, for the full meal. The second worst thing is not ever seeing their faces. I tried FaceTime with Ben once but he squirmed so mightily I decided it was a mistake.

I worry that they feel abandoned in the same way they felt abandoned by their fathers. That they might see this self-exploration as a comment about how I feel about our lives together. I worry they think maybe all these years I've been desperate to escape them and the first chance I got I ran. I worry they don't know that so much of this trip feels like I was pushed into it, like I pushed myself into it, a kid being forced to go to a day camp they didn't choose. So many days I walk, and my footsteps just sound like my boys, my boys, my boys, and here I am exiling myself to this expansive life I don't recognize, with vistas and panoramas, like it's my reward for suffering through them. I worry this is what they think.

After raising them by myself and struggling so hard, I get to live in Europe and *You deserve it!* is all over my Facebook feed. My actual face shows how I deserve this. All day I pretend and all night I dream of them and I want them back and there is no going back ever, ever, ever. I'm here and they are there, and even when I go back, they'll never be there. Not ever. Our home and our habits and our daily patter feels lost for good, and maybe it is. This is the part I never tell anyone, not even me.

And so I told Luca's mother, "I'm flying all of them to Rome in May. We'll all return together." She nodded, grateful and satisfied. She forgave me.

The bike ride is surprisingly quiet and peaceful, all seven of us finding a pace that works and sticking to it in silence for great long stretches along fields of tall grass, just on the outskirts of Rome. Every once in a while, Sergio or Claudio lifts a lazy hand and points to something, calling back the significance of the tree or small fountain we're passing, but their voices are lost on the breeze. The weather called for rain, buckets and buckets of it, so all this warmth and sunshine has come as a wonder to the group. A June day in February, Sergio calls it, and I suspect we're all pretty happy to take a break from being cultural and just enjoy a slow ride along a dirt path on a warm sunny day. I think that if this is all we do for the day it's worth my money for sure. And then we arrive at the old Appian Way and my second cinematic moment in Rome.

It's Claudio and me, two best friends for that space of six hours, standing with our regular people feet on stones where Caesar once walked. The first superhighway in Europe, connecting Rome with the rest of the world. The stones are difficult to ride on, large and round and smooth but inconsistent, and so we try to stay to the sides. Trees bow over each side of the road but are perfectly placed to let in exactly as much dappled light as a person could want. Old gates protect the homes of wealthy people who probably paid millions of dollars just to say their villa backs onto the Appia Antica.

I've been told more than once that I don't know enough about history and I agree. When I chose Rome, I didn't think much about it, simply found something that looked pretty good online and booked before I could talk myself out of it. But I've had a hard time connecting with Rome. With finding that kernel of space where the excited version of me peeks her head out every once in a while. But here she is all of a sudden. Stretched out in the sunshine, sweaty in jeans and a t-shirt. She takes a deep breath and crouches low to touch the stone beneath her feet. The flat of her palm is warm. The other flat of her palm on another stone too, just like that. Just like that I am there. I imagine the feet of soldiers where my hands are, the feet of Caesar. Mark Antony. Perhaps even Cleopatra. Claudio says nothing as I crouch. Doesn't take a picture of some North American woman having her big experience for his Airbnb page. He recognizes something in that moment, a loosening.

Afterwards, we're joined by the others, and I climb on my borrowed bike. I take pictures of Sergio solemnly feeding the cat who lives near the bust of the patriarch of some ancient Roman noble family. We go on to visit the famous aqueducts, still mostly intact, but I'm more interested in the small skirmish Sergio got into with a local picnicker, a young man who seemed to be leaving his McDonald's wrappings behind. Sergio has some choice words for the young man, but he walks away like Sergio hasn't spoken. Shoulders back and chin high.

Handsome and sure of himself, a young adored Roman probably heading home to his mother's house. "See?" Claudio whispers to me as Sergio furiously cleans up after him.

Afterwards, we all go back for a snack called a *suppli*, a deep-fried ball of rice and tomato sauce with warm mozzarella in the middle. "This is the best in Rome," Sergio tells me. And so it is.

Too Many Canadians

Two older Italian women were offering a course in making traditional sauces so I signed up. I wanted to go home with some new skill and this seemed like a good one. They wrote in their ad that they were two cousins who came up with the idea of putting on a cooking class just because they wanted to spend more time together.

I get there a little late after getting lost. I tried the Metro but eventually caved and grabbed a taxi to her apartment. When I finally walk in, they tell me they were worried about me, and they have faces like they mean it. Paola speaks English because she's married to a military man and has travelled all over the world with him. Paola is tall and willowy. She wears her brown hair in a chic bob and a peasant skirt with one of those long, hung belts that don't look good on people except her. Marta does most of the cooking and none of the English-speaking. Marta is no longer married although it's hard to tell if her husband is dead or she's divorced. Either way she seems pretty happy about her single life in her apartment with a view of the opera theatre outside her kitchen window, giddy and relieved when she tells me she's celibate.

The other guests are already there. And they're Canadian. A husband, wife and two surly looking teens. The girl is wearing a baggy sweatshirt and about seven layers of mascara and tight jeans and long fingernails painted a chipped robin's-egg blue. The boy is taller but looks younger, with braces and an eager smile, wearing those nylon running pants that every boy loves at some point in their life and a sweatshirt that fits too big. The whole family looks Italian but they are in fact of Portuguese descent. Mostly though, they're Canadian.

From Toronto, they explain, spending six months travelling Europe. Amy tells me that it's been her dream since she was a girl, and the rest of the family was "game to try anything," although I don't think anyone told her daughter, Talia, this. Within the first five minutes of polite chatter, as we make our appetizers of tiny panzerotti and pizzas, with Marta gently pushing our hands through the dough, Talia loudly says, "Don't you think it's ridiculous that anyone would make their fourteen-year-old daughter come here for six months. Don't you?" Amy doesn't let me answer. She rolls her eyes. "Oh, she's just mad because I made her leave her friends. Tell me wouldn't you have just died to be given the chance to come to Europe for six months when you were fourteen?" I say, "No, not really."

When I was fourteen my friends were absolutely everything in my life. The idea of missing a Saturday night with my friends was a horror when I was a teenager. What if Mike the hockey player was at a party on a Saturday and I missed it? What if that was the night he'd finally kiss me? What if my friends had a sleepover and I couldn't go, and then on Monday they'd have all these secret jokes and I'd be knocked down to second-tier friend? One night was terrible, six months was an impossibility.

Amy wants me to like her, I think, so she agrees with me when I say this. Her daughter pounces, her long talons mashing up the tiny panzerotti she was meant to be preparing on the cookie sheet in Marta's living room. "Can I go home then?" Dan steps in, tall and bald with a mustache and one of those smiles that's meant to show he's long-suffering and patient. "No, obviously not. How would we even get you back? Why don't you just leave your mother alone and get with the program?"

The cooking class is a lot of fun, the recipes not terribly difficult and, if I'm being honest, not much of a revelation. Marta uses tomato sauce from a jar and adds spices like I already did when I was at home. Of course, Marta's sauce is miles better and of course I love it when I'm slowly stirring her puttanesca and she screams at me "*Vy! Vy!*" when I'm not stirring fast enough. This feels like the real deal. I also love watching Paola making *cacio e pepe*, a kind of sauce that is made of Parmigiano cheese and pepper and water and muscles and timing. It takes about ten minutes total, but those ten minutes are a ballet of precision.

After exchanging numbers and leaving class, I try to decide if I like Amy and her family. I know I like Marta and Paola for sure. When we sat down to eat together, Marta spoke to me with Paola's help. She was funny and naughty and drank her red wine with gusto. Paola didn't drink but poured me more and more wine without me having to ask. As for the Canadians, I can't be sure. They're here doing something quite similar, staying in a house on the other side of Rome in a little seaside town called Bracciano. Amy is following her dream to do some self-discovery in Rome like me. And now it looks like we'll have to be friends, like it or not.

I have plans to meet up with a woman from the States later today. We met through a Facebook group called Ladies Social Club Rome Expats. I found it one night after I drank a bottle of pinot grigio and watched the entire first season of *Derry Girls* alone in my studio. That was a Thursday, which meant I was on a 2:00–8:00 shift writing articles for Romper, the website I'd been with for the past three years — a parenting site for millennials — and in my profile photo I wore pigtails and a football shirt for reasons that felt obvious at the time. On days when I work, I get sort of giddy because it means I'm officially off the hook from going out and having madcap adventures. That particular night I was in the cave for too long. I went for a walk in the early morning, got the groceries with my headphones in and my eyes down so I wouldn't have to talk to anyone. I tried to buy fruit but didn't realize I had to weigh it myself and got an incomprehensible earful from the checkout girl. Afterwards I went home and worked and ate and watched TV on my laptop in the same position on my bed. By ten, I realized I hadn't spoken out loud all day and got deeply depressed. I texted a friend from Canada who recommended I find an expat group, and I now I find myself heading to the Piazza del Popolo for my blind date with Lavyrne. We'd made our tentative date via messaging days earlier and providence has me meeting her for real this afternoon. After meeting the Canadians earlier, what a bounty of new friends.

Lavyrne is slick, white teeth and perfect hair. Makeup, leather jacket and a scarf around her neck just so. Her voice has the measured, TV quality of successful Americans or at least Americans who are determined to be successful. We intend to go for a walk but it starts to rain, so we grab a coffee at a bar instead. When I ask her what she does for a living she leans forward and says, "I'm in the business of promotion, do you know what I mean? I'm the person you go to if you have an independent film coming out and you need to get the word out. Or let's say you have a product that people need to know about, you come to me." She pauses while I try to make enthusiastic noises and then asks me what I do. I say I'm a writer but explain I'm not *that* kind of writer, because she gets a quick gleam, like she's going to try to sell me on selling me.

Lavyrne and I drink coffee for two hours. I like her. I like her way of being exactly herself. All slick and careful at first but eventually she peels the edges back. She tells me about her sister who died of cancer the year before and how it was her sister's dream to go to Rome. She came here after her sister passed because she didn't want to end up like that, dying and thinking of the places she could have seen. She's been dating lots of men. "Italian men know how to treat a woman." But she also says they're kind of terrible. She tells me she's a grandmother and I can't believe it. I try not to say it but I really can't. There are young faces and old faces and Botox faces, and hers is a young face.

Afterwards we go to a touristy restaurant with a heated terrace and waiters in tuxedos who hate everyone, I mean they really loathe people. I order a glass of wine in Italian and she orders in Italian too, a burger with fries. "The beef here is the best I've ever tasted," she says, and then boy does she eat that burger with gusto. Lavyrne is bossy and sweet, a good listener and a good talker. She wants me to break up with Nick straight away and tells me that's definitely what I should want too. "You should hear yourself when you talk about him. It's like, *he's great but...*" Lavyrne wants me to be a single woman in Rome like her, luxuriating in all the free dinners the Roman men would certainly want to offer me, she's sure of it. She takes a photo of me drinking my wine in my knitted blue hat with no makeup and a flimsy light-blue scarf from Reitmans tied poorly around my neck and sends it to me with a caption about beauty coming from within. Lavyrne is the kind of friend I want. The kind of friend I'd like even if we weren't in a strange country and glad to speak to someone in our own language. I'd like her normally but, probably because we're away, I love her a lot.

That night I call Nick and tell him about Lavyrne, and I'm giddy. I hear how giddy I am in my voice. "And we're going for a guided walking tour of Rome next week together and Lavyrne says it's just great, even people who don't know about history can follow along, it's so interesting." He's so happy for me but ends his call the same as always. "Geez, I miss you, doll." I forgot to miss him too, just for a second. That's how excited I was about Lavyrne. And I realize how much and how deeply and how desperately I miss the company of women.

Lavyrne and I meet the following week for a walking tour. There's a fellow American who has a well-rehearsed, entertaining script and a disdain for Americans. He tells the eight or so participants at the outset that he'll answer any questions, "but don't ask me about Trump. I've lived here for fifteen years and didn't vote for that asshole." Which means no one really has to ask him about Trump.

Lavyrne and I chat quietly throughout our tour and she's right, it's the best way to see Rome. Our guide has figured out that everyone loves gossip and backstage tidbits, and these are the things he tells us about. A prostitute who was sleeping with all the cardinals in Vatican City and got a street named after her because she was so powerful. The first and only openly gay emperor, Hadrian, who deified his lover after he was rumoured to have been drowned by the Roman Senate. How Queen Margherita (the one the pizza is named for) was essentially the early Roman version of Princess Diana since she was super popular. More popular than her husband even. We stop for gelato and our guide tells us how to order because Romans don't ever line up, and the only pattern I see with Romans is that everyone wants to have the perfect definition for them.

Our tour ends at St. Peter's Basilica, my favourite view, the one I first saw on the back of Tim's Vespa just as the sun set. Lavyrne and I go for a drink and we say our easy goodbyes, new best friends. I sleep better than anything that night.

A few days later Lavyrne has to leave Rome to go back to Florida for a while and doesn't expect to return until I'm gone. Straight women aren't meant to be so shattered by the end of a female friendship but, yes, I'm shattered. Gutted. Alone again but worse, alone after having a person.

I turn to Amy in my sadness. Poor Amy, who has been diligently sending me WhatsApp messages with invitations to stay with her family in their lake house. Recklessly, I tell her I decided to go to Siena for two days and ask if she and her family want to join me.

I'm not surprised when she says yes but I wish I was more excited.

The Mother I Always Wanted

By the time I leave for Siena, I'm starting to wonder if this is a mistake. Amy's emails and messages to me have become increasingly desperate, and I try to understand, I really do. I've been so horribly lonely myself so many times, so desperate for someone to see me. I've exhausted Luca and Angela with my messages about where to get the train schedule and where to order pizza and where to find the best tomatoes, but all my messages are really just *please see me, please, please*. Amy is the same.

She's emailed me about her blog and asked me again and again if I would "have a look" — and that worries me. There's no good ending to having a look at someone's writing. I learned this a week or so earlier when I took part in a writing afternoon with some expats I met on the same Facebook page that brought me Lavyrne. Someone mentioned in a post that it might be a good idea to arrange a writing afternoon in a café in Rome on a Sunday. A chance to meet and write with a group of other women sounded like pure heaven. About six women said they were interested. I'd been scribbling in a pocket-sized journal since I got to Italy and figured I'd just scribble with other people around who might become *my* people if I played my cards right.

The girls were young, all in their early twenties. One was a gorgeous thing from Denmark who had moved to Rome with her equally gorgeous Italian boyfriend, all red lips and perfect hair and a navy jumpsuit cut exactly for her body with a tiny bow in the back. One of the girls made her get up to do a twirl. She smirked when she complied. Another was a poet in a leather jacket who was moonlighting as an au pair and walked in terribly hungover with eyeliner dripping down her face. A few more came, one with social anxiety she talked about like it was a pet on a leash she wasn't sure she'd be able to manage.

I didn't feel like an old lady until we started talking about men in Italy. When I said I thought the Latin Lover Experience was all a rumour and that the men kept to themselves and didn't bother anyone at all, they looked embarrassed. From this, I deduced this wasn't the case for the young and beautiful. They all told stories of being grabbed by a guy at a club or at the McDonald's in line for an order of small fries or by the father of the children they were caring for while in Rome. Being older and invisible suddenly suited me down to the ground.

We sat at the back of a Roman café that could have been anywhere at all, trying to work on our writing. At mismatched tables with local art on the walls and tippy chairs I worried wouldn't support me. Tables too small for laptops, for journals, for cups of coffee and discarded plates of sandwiches. One by one each of them asked me if I wouldn't mind having a look at their poetry. Because I'm older or because I was calmer at that moment, or because I'm a writer, I don't know. "The thing is I don't really know anything about poetry," I said, which was kind of a lie. I understand the big thing about poetry — that it's so personal, the arched brow of a critic can fell you like a tree.

One by one they promised me they wouldn't get upset because one by one they were confident I'd love what they wrote, be in raptures even. And I wish I was the kind of person who could fake raptures, but I can't. I said they could email me their work and then knew I'd never see any of them again. Except for one young woman who worked at the Keats-Shelley House at the foot of the Spanish Steps. She was the only one who never asked me to look at anything, because I suspect she didn't need my approval. I stopped in to see her for an afternoon at the melancholy, beautiful little museum and got a private tour. She directed me to visit the non-Catholic cemetery, and I found Keats's grave marked *Here lies one whose name was writ in water*. We didn't talk much after, but I thought her poetry was probably very fine, too fine for the likes of me to read. As for Amy, it was different. I had a look at her blog before leaving to meet her and her family in Siena. It told me more about her than I wanted to know. For one, she considered herself "the kind of mother I always wanted." And that might be true, but it felt like the sort of thing you're supposed to wait for someone else to say about you.

We booked separate rooms in separate buildings in Siena. Also, separate trains because they decided to go one night earlier. This suited me since I'm happy on a train, always. Happy to stare out the window or close my eyes or write or read as long as I'm on a train, especially alone. The sun was shining when I left for Siena from my preferred station, Roma Tiburtina, which is smaller and has better cafés than Termini.

At Roma Tiburtina I buy a small ham panini and a cappuccino, which they allow me to take out. I miss walking around with a coffee, so this feels special. I have only one change where I hop from one train to another at a tiny platform in a town meant only for train hopping. The owner of the Airbnb where I'll be staying gave me excellent directions to his place, which is right in the centre of the oldest part of the city. I rented a small room on the third floor with big windows that open wide over the rooftops — no cave for me here. I breathe and I breathe.

About twenty minutes after I get in, Amy sends me a message to let me know they're ready to meet me whenever I'm ready, but I'm not ready. I'm talking to my Airbnb host, who is the son of the man who owns this townhouse, and getting directions to a restaurant in the famous town square where he tells me I'm sure to eat the best Tuscan bean soup with bread that exists on the planet. For a minute I have a mean thought, just to be by myself here. For a minute I want to go eat soup and walk around until the sun sets, then find a place for pizza and just see what happens. For a minute I want to let that family of four go off and do whatever they want to do, but I can't do it. I imagine what it would feel like for Amy, to have someone cancel on her when she seems to be flailing a little, and I can't do it. So, I meet them near the Duomo di Siena, which apparently is even nicer than the one in Florence, according to Tim, and we walk around for two hours. We stop in stores sometimes, Amy wanting to buy souvenirs that I can't afford, so I try out my fledgling Italian instead. In Siena, my Italian sounds just great, better than in Rome. It's just enough to coax a smile, just enough for people to tell me I'm doing great when I apologize for my terrible Italian. My favourite sentence is "I'm so sorry, my Italian isn't very good" because it always prompts compliments.

Siena is quiet (like most places in February), the Piazza del Campo ringed with sidewalk pizza places that are sitting empty. No one seems to care, no one misses the tourists. Not that I can see. We stop at the restaurant suggested by my host, where I have that Tuscan bean soup and rustic bread, and it really is the best thing I've eaten in ages. Sausage and good tomatoes and beans and spice and a great curl of Parmesan resting on top. Amy and Dan's kids sit at a different table and drink Coke and eat lasagna. Their son's eye never leaves the gelato menu. I feel such affection for him then. I think of my boys, who were never full, who were always looking for their next feeding, and for one moment I'm fine with where I am, and I'm fine with where they are.

Afterwards we walk some more and stop at a place on the edge of the piazza to watch the sunset. We find a heated terrace where we are fed olives and cheese and bread and wine by the friendly proprietor, even though we didn't order them. He explains he wants to be nice to the tourists in February but not June and we all sort of laugh, except Amy. After he leaves, she tells me with a tight face that she's getting so sick of Italians. So sick of the way no one seems to appreciate the tourists here. She's almost crying by the time she finishes her little speech, bitter tears in her eyes when she says, "I've wanted to come here my whole life and every time I have to deal with an Italian they wreck it." Dan smiles at me apologetically. Her daughter hunches into her seat and rolls her eyes. Then finally Amy mutters, "It's like the goddamn immigrants at home always desperate to get a free ride."

The window is open, the drapes pushed aside. I've seen what's inside Amy's heart. All I can do is ride it out until the next day when I can take the train home.

A Puppy in a Room of Cat People

"No one here likes me." This is what I tell Callum during our Facebook chat. I tell him this when I should be asking him how his life is going and how he and his girlfriend are faring and how his screenplay is coming. I should do a lot of things but I just can't do them. I should feel better by now, I tell him. I should have broken the Italians down and forced them to like me. "You know people like you, Mom," he replies. "You're just homesick." This is what I told nine-year-old Callum when we left my husband.

Callum became a man before he was ever supposed to be a man. No matter how many times I told him he didn't have to be a man, he did it just the same.

There is this photo of the five of us from the time we became the five of us, from a photo shoot in the forest of Harrison Park in Owen Sound. I can't stand to look at it, even now. I can't stand to see the way two-year-old Nathan is clinging to me with his little brow furrowed, or the way three-year-old Jack clutches his Beanie Baby dog with a fake smile on his face, or the way seven-year-old Ben leans a little away from me as we all sit perched on a log. Like he doesn't trust me to get it right. But mostly I can't look at Callum, standing solidly behind me with his back straight and his chin up. His blonde hair like duck fluff; he was still so young. His hands flat on my shoulder blades as I sat in front of him, like *I'll take care of her.*

At the time, he was struggling to make friends, and I told him he was just homesick, but this was a lie. The truth was that he had four years in another school in a bigger town with different lyrics and he'd have to learn the lyrics to the small-town songs or he'd never fit. The truth was, he'd eventually fit. And the truth was, he'd never fit. Like me.

I've been trying to fit in Italy and I'm not fitting. I don't know their lyrics. I fit with Luca and Angela but they have lives they need to live without me. Friends they want to have without me. That day, all those years ago, I lied to nine-year-old Callum and told him everything would be better. I needed things to be fine for him then, needed to believe he wouldn't be bullied when he was for sure. Needed to believe our small-town life would be better even if we didn't have a car or money or friends or any idea about hockey (the currency of local conversation).

I say, "I'm sorry" from another continent. From so far away. I've said this to him so many times and I've meant it every time, but he was just so tired of forgiving me when he wasn't mad at me in the first place. Usually, he tells me it's fine, but this time during our Facebook chat Callum just says, "Why don't you head to France a little early?" I was meant to be in Italy for another week or so but, yes, I decide on a dime. Yes, I'm allowed to leave early. I think, *I've had my fill of Italy, or Italy has had enough of me.* I think, *Maybe it's not Italy's fault that I'm not fitting in. I'm missing the boys too much to be happy anywhere.* But still I feel that tingling of freedom. Like someone's just come along and said, "You're free to go," when I thought I was chained to a tree. Cal says, "I don't know why you went to Italy for so long in the first place, we both know you wanted to go to France more." He's right, it's always been going to France for me. The south of France specifically.

So, I buy my ticket, and I go to France early. Because why not?

Mais Catastrophe

I take the train from Tivoli to Rome and a train from Rome to
the airport and fly to Marseille and take the hour-long train to
Avignon and catch a taxi to 22 rue Notre-Dame in Avignon.
But my new studio isn't at 22 rue Notre-Dame in Avignon.

It's four days before I'm supposed to arrive. My new
landlady, Liza, has allowed me to come early, she said so
in an email. And now here I stand on a street with a bar
called Bar and a small supermarket dappled with light
graffiti, but no studio rented by me. Also there's a pizza
place. Of course, there's a pizza place. It seems there's no
escaping pizza for the rest of my life, even at the airport in
Rome, where I accidentally dropped a slice of hot pizza on
the head of a small French girl, and her father screamed,
"Mais catastrophe!" like I was a criminal. Pizza will always
be with me, I fear.

This pizza place, the kind where most people take food
home so they don't have to stay too long under the buzzing
fluorescent lights, is the true north star of the street as the sun
goes down. I stand with my purple suitcase and my shoulder
bag and my laptop bag and my coat on the corner. Everything
else is darkness now that the supermarket has rolled down its

heavy-duty security door for the evening. I call Nick, ready to cry. Ready for him to solve my problems.

"It's okay, doll, try to calm down," he answers. "I've looked up your new place on Google Street View and it's definitely inside the ramparts, I think you must be lost. Hold on while I figure it out." I tell him I tried to call Liza but the number clicked off before connecting. I tell him I was stupid to book anything on a website I don't know, because what if it's all a ruse? He tells me to calm down again and I want to remind him that no one in the history of hysteria has ever calmed down when told to calm down. Before I can lash out, he calms me down. "Your street is rue Notre-Dame des Sept Douleurs, doll. You just forgot to give the taxi driver the last part of the name." When I spoke to the taxi driver, I was in this dream state between Italian and French. I studied Italian so hard for two months that it pushed all my French (and some of my English) out of me and so I blustered my way through. Apologizing. I can apologize in all languages, even with my eyebrows only. But I didn't remember to give him my full address.

Nick tells me to call the taxi company and have someone come get me and so I do. I let him off the line back in Canada even though I can barely stand it. I call the taxi company and they tell me they'll come get me but this is a lie. I stand there with my tilting purple suitcase and my throbbing right ankle from where the wheels have been knocking against it all day and I stare in vain down the road to the left and right. Afraid to move and afraid to call Nick again and afraid I've made another mistake because I felt I deserved a trip I probably don't deserve.

And then the men from the bar start to filter out in shifts. They've been gazing at me through the window across the street the entire time as though I'm a TV show they can't decide if they want to watch or not. Four of them plus the bartender, and all of them old and lined with moustaches, all leaning on their elbows silently. I think about what they're seeing, leggings and messy hair and too much luggage and a face frozen in the kind of panic that gives a woman wrinkles. At first, one comes out to smoke a cigar, the thin fragrant kind I feel certain is dipped into some sort of delicious port wine or brandy. He stands on the other side of the street looking at me but doesn't approach. The next comes out but goes back in when I won't look his way. Finally, the bravest of the group comes out to stand in the middle of the street, peering in the darkness to look for my taxi with me. Acting as if he knows what I'm after.

I smile at him tentatively and he immediately says, "*Ça va, madame?*" I tell him no, I'm lost. My taxi left me here and my French is bad and I don't know how to get where I'm going. By the end of my sentence, two of his friends have wandered out to join us in the street and then we're all pulling my suitcases into the bar where I'm told to sit down and drink a small glass of cold rosé. They ask me if I'm American, like everyone does. I say I'm Canadian, and one man says, "Oh, I was going to guess Swedish," leaving me inexplicably flattered. I tell them I'm quite lost, that I rented a place online and if I could just find Wi-Fi I could contact my landlady. One man runs, actually runs, across the street to ask the pizza vendor for his Wi-Fi password, but he can't remember it. The whole time I'm sitting at this long bar (shiny like a mirror and made of some kind of wood) petting the dog of one of these men. "*Chien,*" he says to me out of the blue. "Do you know? Woof, woof?" I tell him yes and smile, but he doesn't smile back.

Finally, I show one of the men the address and he says, "Oh, I know this place very well!"

They're getting ready to finish their beers and take a road trip with me and my luggage when I remember the dialling code for France is different because of the extra zero. I call Liza and this call goes through. She has the sort of trilling, melodic voice that is at once mocking and full of empathy. Sweet and dark. She tells me to stay where I am and she'll come get me right away. The news deflates my new friends at the bar who were looking forward to an adventure. Their smiles slide into grimaces, and I decide to stand outside to wait for Liza.

Outside their voices drift to me. They think I don't understand but I understand just fine, like everyone does when they know someone is talking about them. One man says he thinks I'm kind of pretty, another doesn't agree. He says I'm too old for him. Too old to give him babies, he says, and I can't fault him since he's right. Finally, a soft voice in the background says, "I barked like a dog for her. Do you hear me? I barked like a dog." A few voices say, "Yes, we heard that for sure." And on they go with the rest of their night.

Liza is a friend to me immediately when she roars up in her chic Fiat 500. She wears a fuchsia top and a silk scarf of pale purples around her neck, and I wonder if she stopped to touch up her lipstick before coming to rescue me, it looks so fresh. She's dark-haired with dark eyes and beautiful bone structure. I'm immediately a little bit in love with her. She drives just like the kind of person who'd want to drive a Fiat 500, fast and reckless. My French is rusty but she's someone I understand right away. In the car she quickly apologizes for not getting me from the train station but explains that parking in Avignon is impossible and she can't give up her space at night. I would eventually know this is absolutely true. We drive to Porte Thiers, turn a slight right and there we are parked in front of my new studio. My new home.

Inside, the walls are pale yellow and everything else is white except a distressed blue-green wardrobe that leans against one wall and is big enough to fit all my clothes. There's a table with two bamboo ladder-back chairs and a vase with flowers and a small tablecloth with Liza's initials monogrammed on it. A futon made up with teal cotton sheets and several pastel blankets and artwork on the walls (black-and-white vintage photos of Avignon) and a bookshelf of books and a turntable with French records. A small kitchen with a cooktop and one of those half fridges where she's put a little puréed zucchini soup, some milk, coffee, bread and chocolate. She shows me my room and tells me she lives upstairs, and even though it's ten o'clock at night, I ask her where I can buy some wine. Later she tells me this was when she knew I'd be a friend.

She gives me directions to the grocery store around the corner, called Carrefour City. The walk takes ten minutes and I pass a small fountain and thin, tall houses in different shades of cream with window boxes of flowers and herbs. The street cafés are full of people drinking wine and eating dinner. Gesturing, always gesturing, smiling my way as I race to the market for my bottle of wine and cheese and, okay, maybe a baguette even if it is a little stale at that time of night. When I come out with two bottles of wine, one for each hand, a table of three men laugh and clap for me when I hold them up in triumph.

Avignon is alive. It's just so alive. And so am I.

On Giving Up

When I was thirty-three, I gave up. It was a Friday in the summer and I just couldn't keep going anymore so I took the phone off the hook and I crawled into bed and I gave up. I was working at a restaurant called Joe Tomato's where I had to make two choices every week: work shifts where I made enough money to support my family or work shifts where I could raise my family. If I worked nights, I made double the tips, but my kids had to sleep at my aunt's house and the kids didn't like it, Cal and Ben especially. They didn't want to be in a different house at night. Ever. When I called my aunt's house from work to say goodnight to the boys, she could never find them, not ever. She'd tell me they were out riding their bikes with their friends and I'd think, *This isn't okay. If I were home, the boys would be on the couch with me and maybe I'd read Jack and Nathan a story and then put them to bed. Maybe afterwards, Cal and Ben and I would make popcorn and watch* Survivor *together.* I thought, *I could finish my laundry and clean up the kitty litter, prep lunches, read a book.*

Instead, I asked her to call me when Callum and Ben got back from wandering the streets. They were twelve and eleven and the silence on the other end of the phone where their voices should have been felt like a warning. *You're doing it wrong, you're doing it wrong. It's all going to go so wrong.* I knew how their story could turn out, all the time in Owen Sound I saw how these stories turned out. Single mom, too many kids, working nights. No supervision, no control, no hope. If I didn't watch them, if I just let the tide take them, like I saw so many other kids get taken in our town, I would have failed at the only thing I actually cared about passing.

I tried working during the day at Joe Tomato's for a while, the 10:30–4:00 shift that always turned into the 10:30–2:30 shift because business died down immediately after lunch. I was a bartender but also got a section of tables for lunch eaters. Teachers coming in to split clubhouse sandwiches with sides of tomato tortellini soup, and men who worked at the car dealerships down the highway eating steak sandwiches and french fries. Or maybe they went with the panzerotti stuffed with green peppers and pepperoni and mushrooms and onions, the deluxe number 4. I had a few regulars who would come in, sit at the bar to eat their lunch and drink a pint of Molson Canadian or Keith's Pale Ale before heading back out to fix a broken toilet or finish a drywall job or wire someone's new basement rec room. Lunches went quickly and efficiently.

I worked with another waitress named Kathleen most days. She and I liked our coffees together before the rush of customers as we rolled sets of forks and knives into their little paper napkin beds, and prepared mason jars for Bloody Caesars with spicy celery rims. We were both moms, both loved talking about our kids, and it could have all worked out if I made more than twenty dollars in a shift. For Kathleen, the money wasn't as important. She'd been a stay-at-home mom until her youngest daughter started school, then she decided to go back to work to keep busy in the hours when her family was out of the house. For me it wasn't enough. I could pick my kids up from school but I couldn't fill our cupboards with food. I could be there to keep an eye on them in the evenings, making sure they were doing their homework and emptying their backpacks of the apples they refused to eat, which sat softly spoiling in the folds under some crumpled papers. I could stay on top of signing their permission slips but I couldn't pay for their field trips. We lived in a house that was sinking me every day. A four-bedroom century home on the river, four blocks from school and around the corner from the farmers market and the library. It was perfect for us in all the ways we couldn't afford. The rent was higher than I'd ever paid on my own and the heat even worse. When winter came, the little boys always had runny noses, even when I made them wear their slippers and sweaters in the house. I had locked in a one-year lease because I was sure something would get better. Back then, I was only two years out of my marriage and I really believed we were just around the corner from good things. So positive I was the kind of person who would make things better because I believed, then, that I was meant for more, that we were meant for more. I was a waitress still, but not really. Not in the way I thought other people were waitresses, where they didn't look beyond that shift or their day off or the reservations on a Saturday night when busloads of hockey families would be coming in to fill the banquet room fifty at a time. These were commas in my life, brief pauses I'd move past eventually because the boys and I were something special together.

Then, when I was thirty-three, I stopped believing it. I couldn't make things happen for us anymore. My rent was dangerously late, more than two months, and the $200 here and there I'd offer my landlady was no longer keeping her at bay. She needed all the rent or we'd have to go. She told me in June, just as the boys were getting ready for the summer. Just as I was facing eight weeks of arranging visits with their fathers during school holidays. Two sets of boys going to each dad for a court-mandated two-week visit. Both had new babies with new partners then. A baby girl for Mark, Callum and Ben's dad, and a baby boy for David. I'd listen to my sons talk about their babies and compare notes at the breakfast table. Jillian was crawling at Mark's house, but Cody was getting ready to take his first steps. Cody liked his bath, and Jillian had bright-red hair. They loved them so. Jack was just a little boy and already had this paternal love for Cody. Nathan liked having a younger sibling. With their fathers, their lives sounded like clean floors and security and new beginnings; with me, they might not even have a home to come back to.

I stopped sleeping at night around that time, a bout of insomnia hitting me harder than it had done years earlier when I left David, when it was the end of my love for my husband that kept me up at night. Something that felt saccharine sweet to me now. Self-serving. Petty. Now, my insomnia was fuelled by my kids. My sons who trusted me to raise them and I just wasn't doing it. We had our car repossessed because I couldn't pay the loan on time. We were living in a house that looked beautiful on the outside and was rotting on the inside, infested with mice and even a mole. Bad spirits frightened the boys and saw them sleeping in heaps of blankets and pillows around my room. Jack's birthday came and went without a party and with my gifts of things like sandals and shorts and one small toy. This was the one year his dad bought him actual presents, and Jack itemized them to me when he came back, the relief on his face as he clutched his new Game Boy. It was like taking a bullet to the chest for me.

My friends noticed things were bad but would say things like "Aren't the dads ever going to chip in for anything?" And to them, this was the end of the conversation. I should just make their fathers pay the child support they were told to pay by the courts. One dad paid a little and the other paid exactly sixty-five dollars a month, which I told myself I'd turn down out of pride every time but I never turned it down once, not ever.

I got desperate when my landlady told me I'd have to go. Imagined trying to come up with first and last month's rent, imagined explaining to new landlords that I'd take care of their house as my four sons and my rescue dog and my not-neutered cat lined up behind me. Already I had to lie to get this house by saying I had only two sons and that I was working things out with my husband. It bothered me in a way that lying doesn't bother me. I asked my mother if the boys and I could move in with her, something she'd been asking me to consider for years. She lived in Barrie at the time, two hours away from Owen Sound. A town where my brothers lived, where I'd worked for years and still had friends. *I could go back to school maybe*, I thought. *Consider getting that teaching degree I wanted.* My mom and my stepdad lived in a big house with a fenced-in backyard that would be good for our dog, Lily — if she let me keep Lily. I could work out the details as they came along but the point was, I could make a better life for us there. I was sure of it. I had to be sure of it. I needed to be sure of it.

My mom told me it wasn't possible. She said I'd have to figure it out for myself. She said, "You've made your bed, honey, you're just going to have to lie in it." She loaned me her car to get back to Owen Sound for that weekend as a consolation prize. I dropped the boys off with their dads so I could work double shifts for a week while they were gone. Mark met us at the McDonald's in Collingwood, our usual halfway point, and when he got out of the car, a cute black dog came bounding out behind him, and Callum and Ben screamed, "A puppy! Yay! Thanks, Dad!" I stopped feeling anything then. I didn't know why but I did. I drove myself home. I took the phone off the hook. And I didn't move again for three days.

I didn't know that giving up was a thing you could do, but it turns out you can. It turns out a person can give up on their life and probably no one will even know. In the beginning of my giving up, when I lay in my bed crying softly with my dog, Lily, licking my face, I thought something might happen. I was numb with waiting for the reckoning, for the big moment when someone would knock on my door to check on me. It never came. I was scheduled to work a ten-hour shift at the restaurant on Friday. That night I thought someone from work might come to knock on my door to yell about how they were short-staffed and accuse me of leaving the rest of the servers in the weeds all night. I lay there, not sleeping, with *Bridget Jones's Diary* playing on a loop on my DVD player. My heart pounding in my throat. Waiting to ignore the knock. Nothing. I was scheduled to work on Saturday from 11:00 a.m. until after the late-movie crowd from the cinema next door to the restaurant died down and on Sunday for the brunch-and-matinee crowd. No one came.

I want to tell you that I thought about my kids, but I didn't. I thought about nothing. I lay there in my pyjamas and my cardigan with a fan blowing on my face and I went away. It didn't feel bad at all. Sometimes, even now, I try not to think about how easy it was to slip away; how nothing hurt.

How my world didn't go dark but just a sort of beige. Ecru even. I thought I might die then. I wasn't sure how, but I thought it just might happen if I lay there resting long enough. I could just slip away easy as anything. The kids would be fine with their dads and my friends would barely notice my absence. I was just another face in the mix to them, to everyone. I was always the person to beg for visits, beg for attention from the kids and my family and my friends. It might even be a relief. I thought it would be a relief to everyone. Especially me. Not in a way that made me feel sorry for myself but in a way that gave me permission to leave. *You won't be hurting anyone. They'll be fine.* Well, everyone except my dog, I guess. Lily had to go outside to pee and was really terrible at having accidents in the house. I must have let her out because there were no accidents, I just don't remember. This was the only miracle of those three days.

By Sunday night I stopped feeling hungry. The TV I had pulled into my bedroom for movie nights with the kids stayed on. I stared at it with dry eyes that stung when they were closed and stung when they were open. I didn't die though. You can give up for three days, but it won't kill you. You'd have to do something to make it kill you and I couldn't even do that.

On Monday I decided to get up. I had failed at giving up. This was how it was to me then. This was how I saw it. An embarrassment. I was weak and I figured I was hungry again and I wanted to talk to someone. I called my aunt. We went to Cotton Ginny at the mall and got takeout Chinese food, the mall kind where you get to pick three choices with your rice or noodles. I got sweet-and-sour chicken balls, Szechuan beef and mixed vegetables. We watched a movie at her house, *Bring It On*, I think.

On Tuesday I called work and apologized. They told me
they figured something must have happened with the boys,
no problem. No problem at all, we covered your shifts for
you, but you need to come in tonight, okay? I went in that
night like they told me. Maybe I thought giving up would
make something happen for me, but it didn't. Maybe I
thought it would be like *Indiana Jones and the Last Crusade*
when he has to step onto a bridge that isn't there, his eyes
closed, using his faith only. Maybe I thought if I gave up, I'd
step off a bridge and there would suddenly be something
underneath my foot to keep me from falling. There wasn't
and then there was.

About two weeks after I gave up, I came to the house (it
was still my home for one more month) to find a package at
the door. I'd just picked the kids up from their subsidized day
camp at the YMCA, all of them quiet with their own stories.
The package wasn't from a creditor like I first thought. It was
a small homemade lasagna and a bottle of wine and a fifty-
dollar bill and some chocolate. The note read, *Dear Jen, I just
think you should know you're doing a great job. Keep going!
Your friend.* I don't know who wrote this note, even now. I
don't know who cooked that lasagna or who curled that fifty
dollars around the small clear bag of chocolates. What I'm
telling you here is that I don't know who saved me. Because
they saved me for sure.

The Climb

In the Place de l'Horloge in Avignon, an old carousel sits under the shade of the Palais des Papes. It's a neat little square where tourists come to eat lunch and look at the carousel and it's the first place I found a croissant in France. I'd eaten lots of croissants in Ontario and even in Quebec, but this is my first real French croissant, in a café painted all in red with black-and-white checkered floors. I order my croissant and a café crème and say, "This is the first croissant I've eaten in Europe in twenty-five years," and my waiter says, "Okay." That's when I remember, not everyone cares about every thought I have. I sit by the window watching people walk by, writing nothing in my journal except that this croissant isn't as good as I hoped.

The Palais des Papes is easy to find because of the gleaming gold statue looking down on everyone, either Jesus or Mary or the pope, I'm not sure. On the other side of the Palais des Papes is the bridge we all know about, the broken one where everyone was dancing either on or under, no one is quite sure. Overlooking the Pont d'Avignon is a park that was built on top of an old stone jail called Rocher des Doms, and here is where I find my stride. Here is where things change for me.

I'm someone who climbs. Stairs and hills but not walls, because I don't have the equipment or the knowledge or the upper-body strength. I climb because I don't like speed walking and I've heard I'm too old to start running. I climb outside because I don't like the smell of gyms and I want the people who see me to think I'm going places. I climb because a few years ago I lost enough weight that I could fit my bottom into my airplane seat and I want to keep it that way.

Avignon is flat everywhere, a city that runs in tight little circles on streets lined with plane trees bowing gently over sidewalk cafés. But then there's Rocher des Doms. There are two hundred stairs from the bottom to the top, wide stone stairs that curve around a mossy green hill that takes you to the very top where you can see the Alpilles in the distance and the deep-green Rhone flowing below. From the top, you can see the ferry boat that crosses between Avignon and l'île de la Barthelasse, full of cyclists and walkers who want to look at Avignon from the other side of the river. I can tell you the Rhone smells better on that side, but I can't tell you why.

I find Rocher des Doms on my second day in Avignon. Liza comes downstairs to my studio in a flurry of fast French that I don't quite understand, telling me she's going to show me around. I understand when she tells me she doesn't always do this for people. I understand I'm meant to feel a bit special and a bit irritating and so I do. We whip around in her Fiat 500 with the windows down, her gesturing with both hands at the scenery so confidently, I'm not nervous that she almost never touches her steering wheel. We see all the sights that mean something to her; her old house in Villeneuve-lès-Avignon and the good supermarket she likes and the little farm where she buys eggs sometimes and comes to pet the donkey (he looks like he doesn't understand her French all the time either). After we drive along the outside of the ramparts (stay inside the walls, she tells me, outside the walls is only for the unfortunate people), I spot Rocher des Doms. "What's up there?" I ask. An old jail we're trying to turn into a park, Liza tells me. And so begins my daily climbing ritual in Avignon and the life I decide to start for myself there. A life that doesn't seem worth sharing with anyone really but feels worthy just to me.

The next morning, I lace up my running shoes and walk along the outside of the ramparts. It's about 9:30 a.m. and the Rhone flows on past with a few rowers and a houseboat giving off the scent of some sort of sweet wood smoke I don't recognize. The houseboat has laundry hanging on a makeshift line under a red-and-white awning, a coffee cup on the table and a newspaper lying beside it. There's a small boat with the words Boat School in French written across the front and a one-story white café with bright-blue trim boasting it's been overlooking the river there since 1929. Inside, men are playing cards and drinking coffee; a scooter and an impossibly small car that looks like it was from the seventies are parked at the side. The men glance up at me when I walk by and one nods hello. At the base of Rocher des Doms, I start climbing the stairs. There's an iron gate partway up and a view of the river when I turn left, another view of it when I turn right. At the top, I walk through the little park where there's a grotto and yet another café and a fountain and trees with rows and rows of herbs growing just outside the walls of the Palais des Papes. There's a small girl of about two being slowly walked around the courtyard by her father, the two of them holding hands and talking to each other with their heads bowed. I go down the stairs and then pivot on my heel and I climb them again. And again. Eight times in total. I wear my baseball cap and a sweatshirt and leggings and listen to "My Favorite Murder." Other people are climbing too, young men with strong legs who run past me two at a time and don't say a word. One couple climbs the stairs alongside me on my third lap, he in loose track pants and a t-shirt, she in bright-pink running pants and a Just Do It sweatshirt. At the top we look at each other and smile in that way that says, *Can you believe we just did that?*

A few days later, I'm walking the same path. I pass by the same café and the same men are playing the same game of cards, I think. One of them nods at me again, but this time with a little tip-of-the-hat motion because I'm really hustling. I smile and so does he. At the top of the stairs a man sits with a cane — and a bag of breadcrumbs for pigeons. He's stretching his legs out in the sun, wearing a perfectly correct jacket, trousers and scarf despite the warmth. He isn't reading or listening to music. He doesn't feed the pigeons even though they coo at his feet. He just stares straight ahead with a look of such pure contentment on his face that it hitches my breath a little. He's the same every time I pass him, except the last time, when I stand with my hands on my knees and can't breathe. He does a short little applause without looking at me. I think it's for me. I'm pretty sure it's for me.

For one month, I climb these stairs at least five days a week, sometimes bringing along a little money to take a coffee at the top when I'm finished. I see disco yoga classes on Sundays, and other days there are young couples straddling the ledge, French kissing very poorly. I walk in rain and sun and wind; the wind is the absolute worst. Sometimes I walk home through town to buy bread from the boulangerie I like. I always meet people who smile at me and make eye contact. I can't tell you why, but those stairs are where I make a life for myself in France. They are the starting point for something that looks like self-awareness.

Maybe I'm not adventurous. Maybe I just want a new kind of sameness. Maybe that's okay.

Black Leggings:
The Last Line of Defence

Four months in Europe means four periods, a thing I didn't consider before I left Canada. The first time I got my period in Tivoli I was flummoxed. I'm always surprised when I get my period, even now that I'm in my forties, always going back over my mood swings and sore breasts and hunger and facial breakouts from the previous few days like I'm reconstructing a crime scene I probably should have known was coming all along. But in Tivoli it was worse. I didn't pack any pads or tampons and I usually need both. Maybe because I gave birth four times or maybe because I had a tubal when Nathan was six weeks old or maybe because a heavy flow is a genetic thing in my family, I don't know. We don't talk much about periods in our family, even though people talk to me about their gastrointestinal issues a lot more than I'd like. "It was coming out both ends of me, you should have seen it!" was a popular conversation opener with the McGuire men and women always. Periods, on the other hand, were not.

When I woke up in Tivoli, in January, with that awful low feeling in my stomach and realized my period had come yet again, I had no idea where to buy pads or tampons. I hadn't yet found the supermarket where the cashiers and I would stage an ongoing war over the pronunciation of the Italian word for *shopping bag* that they seemed to change on me constantly. I only knew about the local grocer: the man up the hill from my house who ran a popular deli that sold bread and olives and clementines, wine and beer, cleaning supplies and tissue paper. He seemed to have one of everything. So I did the thing every woman has done everywhere. I balled up some wadded toilet paper and prayed it would do the trick. I ran up the hill to his store. I didn't know the word for *tampon* in Italian and I wouldn't have used it if I did. Already, I noticed in Italy a disdain for female needs, like toilet seats and private washrooms where a person might, say, reapply some lipstick. I imagined there'd be little patience in this deli for my feminine needs — and I was right.

The man who ran the grocery had nothing to say to me as usual, and as usual, it hurt my feelings more than it should have. Probably because I'm the kind of person who wants to become friends with service staff all the time and usually it's at least politely received. But this man behind the counter, clenching an unlit, half-smoked cigarette between his teeth, was making himself a sandwich with three kinds of cured meat and some thick focaccia bread slathered in butter. I looked at the top of his bald head — the kind of bald where obscene pubic hairs peeked up out of his scalp — and I really hated him for a minute. Standing there, potentially bleeding through my wadded up toilet paper with my black leggings as my last line of defence against total shame, I really hated him for not looking up.

I made a lot of noise banging around his store, smacking into a stack of brightly coloured sponges so the neat three-packs scattered on the ground. I picked up all but one package, out of spite. He could pick it up himself later. I got ready to buy a bottle of wine for two euros and some salami and some salad greens. And I couldn't find the feminine hygiene products anywhere. More men who were exactly the same as the owner came in and more men ignored me. I looked through the toilet paper section and there was nothing. I found the baby diapers and baby wipes but no tampons. In Canada, supermarkets always put diapers and maxi pads together, which sends me two messages — either *Look at you, a grown woman wearing a maxi pad and it's disgusting*, or *Don't need pads? Guess what, you probably need diapers because you're pregnant*.

Guess where I found them finally? Hidden on a top shelf behind the Italian version of Comet and the toilet-cleaning solutions. There was a wobbly plastic stool provided discreetly beside the shelves so women could reach up for their shame products without asking for help, and while they were at it, they might want to remember to get some cleaning supplies for their afternoon of housework. Once I was up on that stool, that's when the men glanced my way with looks of frustration and mild disgust. I bought my products in an unreasonably thick silence where it felt like everyone had stopped breathing from the shock of my behaviour and I thought, *I hope I don't get my period next month*, but of course, I did. This train isn't stopping for me just yet.

The next month was the same because I didn't buy enough products. I went to the supermarket that was mostly like a supermarket from home except they seemed to feel the same about periods there, even the women. Again, the products were hidden with the cleaning supplies and again when I bought them, the cashier looked horrified. Genuinely horrified, even more than when I tried to buy bananas without weighing them first (that was a real scandal at the local Todis). She didn't even ask me if I needed a bag this time, she just gave me one for free and put my tampons and maxi pads in the bag herself without looking me in the eye. This was a woman of thirty-five, who has presumably had a period at least once.

And that's why my third period in France is a love story. It's the moment when I realize, *I could live here, actually live here, in a way I've never lived anywhere.* You might think this is an exaggeration but this is the truest thing. I walk to the Carrefour City on rue Carnot, pulling my wheeled grocery cart on loan from Liza. I'm not yet on my period but, for once, I decide I won't be surprised by it. I'll be ready even if my period descends on me in the dead of night. At the Carrefour City, I buy a prepared salad with greens and some sort of mustard balsamic dressing, little garlic toasts topped with chèvre and olives and sundried tomatoes. I buy two bottles of rosé, since they're on sale, and some dark chocolate with bits of orange peel and a small expensive jar of organic carrot soup made with coconut milk, yogourt, berries, a nutty granola, some honey and coffee and milk and mineral water. I have that wheeled grocery cart filled to the brim with foods purchased for me and me alone, and it still feels like a revelation three months into my trip. Then I cap it all off with a special treat for myself, tampons *and* maxi pads bought from a well-lit wall entirely of feminine products. I even buy the super-plus kind I need, why not? Nobody here knows me. They're placed on shelves beside shampoo and nail clippers and toilet paper and moisturizer. Bathroom essentials. What a concept.

When I go up to the cashier, a young girl with a waterfall of dark hair in high-waisted jeans and a cropped loose turtleneck with a hint of lipstick, I hesitate for a second. As a grown woman, I still hesitate, not because of the Italian men from my last experience buying these products but because of a lifetime of hiding the fact that I get my period. I get over myself and, of course, she doesn't care. Of course. She scans the products, and we talk about the chocolate I'm buying. She thinks it's good but not as good as a salted-caramel one she tells me I should try next.

After I drop my groceries at the studio, I walk to watch the sunset over the Rhone. I walk the long curve of the ramparts under the plane trees beside the wide, wide Rhone. There are women everywhere, for the first time I see this. Two women in trench coats walk arm in arm and talk to no one but each other. Looking at no one but each other, this isn't a moment for audience participation. Two women that look about my age and just about like the kind of women I'd want to be friends with are out for a run. One stops running for a second to double over laughing, slapping at her friend who keeps saying all the good things she's obviously been saying. University students look separately at their phones but walk together with their oversized scarves and matching hair. I plug my headphones into my phone and listen to "La Vie En Rose" as the sun sets over the Pont d'Avignon, the famous bridge, over the plane trees and the long grass and the cobblestone walkway. I listen to Django Reinhardt, Dalida and Édith Piaf, all the clichés. I keep my sunglasses on even after the sun goes down, even after I find a spot to sit on the small ferry dock. The street lamps come on and cast that flattering pale-yellow glow on the trees and on the river and on me. I cry like I haven't cried in a long time. I cry like I've found a place that's meant for this one little corner of me, the one from before the boys, which apparently, is still here after them as well.

There was this girl inside me, before my boys came to be, a girl who knew I'd live here. Not exactly here, maybe, but somewhere in France, probably Paris. If I could remember where this dream of my future life started, I'd tell you but I don't because it was always there. In grade eight when I was a round girl with a round face and a square hank of hair hanging to my neck, I thought about living in a little apartment above a café. A place where I'd smell the baguettes baking in the early morning. My place was always the same palette of faded bright colours that I now recognize as second-hand chintzy sorts of things. Old poufs in aged reds with gold tassels and bookcases stuffed with books I wanted to read, not books I thought I was supposed to read. Books that felt true or were true only. In my dreams this place had a window over my dining-room table with little flowers in a teacup or a tall thin vase — it changed when I changed with every season and every year. Sometimes there was a terrace but mostly there wasn't, just a bed in the middle of the room and a bathtub so deep even my breasts were covered, not floating around for me to see no matter how hard I tried not to look.

This girl was a writer with no money but had lots of friends who didn't have money either. We ate the kind of cheese where the mould has to be scraped off and maybe croissants from the boulangerie below. The owner would be kind. They would teach me how to bake a baguette to help me save my *centimes*. I'd have a careless wardrobe of artful things that just appeared, scarves for my neck and my hair. Floppy hats for when I didn't want to do my hair. T-shirts with bands I really liked, which were soft and old and kind to my curves.

That was my *before*. What I wanted before my dreams shifted to the sweet smell of babies and little boys in shorts and rubber boots, their cheeks pink with health and sunshine. Then my dreams became warm beds and food on the table made by my two hands, a farm somewhere with bedrooms for everyone and a stream for swimming. That dream I know better than my damn fingers. That dream tortured me but also pulled me forward for years, pulled us forward. That dream was a cool damp face cloth on my fevered forehead when I thought no one noticed I was sick. That dream protected my boys and protected me from hopelessness.

This was *the other*. This was a dream that was older than me, a dream that came from nowhere.

I stand crying under a plane tree, looking out at the Rhone because I thought that girl was gone. I thought she'd never find her way here. I thought she never existed in the first place. And I cry because I remember I have chocolate with orange peel at home waiting for me and wine. At home.

I get my period the next morning. And I'm ready.

Marrying the Ketchups

On Sunday I talk with my mom. In Italy we talked all the time but not in Avignon. It's been almost two weeks. She punched in for a shift of trying to solve my problems every second or third day while I sulked in Tivoli, holding her iPad up to her face and shouting, "Jen? Jen?" to make sure I was still there. I was always still there. I was always waiting for her to feel sorry for me so I could feel sorry for myself. When I was feeling wretched about women who wouldn't embrace me, who wouldn't make eye contact. When I couldn't swallow the loneliness and the worry over my boys, she was there to make all the right soothing noises. She commiserated about the loneliness; she understood from California where she'd been living far away from all of us for years. And as for the women who wouldn't love me, she'd say they were just jealous because I'm beautiful or they were resentful of my blonde hair (which came from a bottle they could easily buy as well). She'd say they were worried I'd steal their men. I believed none of this, but I believe she believes it, even now. I believe she got real, deep joy from trying to fix me. When my boys were little and she was at Walmart buying club packs of Dunkaroos and sandwich meat and a big pot roast to keep in the freezer. The bounty an embarrassment to me. A reminder of everything I wasn't providing. A twenty-dollar bill folded into my coat pocket as a surprise or a gift card for Harvey's and the movie theatre, the words implicit: *I hope you always need me like this. I never want you to stop needing me.*

When I call her from Avignon, my life feels good. Better.

I bought a second-hand bike from a local garage and I take it for a long test drive on l'île de la Barthelasse with Liza and another new friend, Pierre. We eat a late lunch with Pierre's Australian girlfriend, Jeannie, then pack up our bikes on the free ferry to tour the island. Pierre is already like a brother, a pal, someone my age who feels natural, so natural. We like each other even though we didn't choose each other; we were playdates picked out by our shared best friend, Liza. She chose us as her friends, her younger beloveds, and we like these roles very much. We like to be pulled along behind her as two naughty children who happen to be in their forties, who delight her with our sass. We teach her the worst swear word in English, which is obviously *cunt*, and she laughs hysterically and writes it in her phone and says, "Oh, I like that! Cunt! I will use this the next time I drive my car and have problems. Cunt!" She finds us delightful and delicious and full of sunshine. This is what she says to me: "You are full of sunshine." And I want this to be true for her, so it is.

Pierre doesn't have a bike so he jogs easily beside us as we wind our way past the sleepy canal where houseboats are moored. Friends and couples and families all enjoying the bright-blue day on the decks, wearing pastel sweaters loose around their shoulders. One couple lazily lifts their glasses from the deck of their houseboat as we pass, in that slow languid way of Sundays when most everything is closed for shopping. We inhale the sweet smell of peach trees — fields of them in full blossom — before we see them. We ride and ride and barely speak except to say something about our happiness to be doing exactly what we're doing; every once in a while, we do this to make sure we all know. We're happy together. Such a surprise. The roads are flat and dry. Our bellies are full. I go home happy.

I go home feeling the Sundayness of it all. Filled up with the little part-time life I'm building myself, and I want to show it to my mom right away. I want her to be happy for me, but maybe my reasons are also mean and ugly, I don't know for sure. Maybe rubbing my little change purse of happiness in her face will be mean and ugly when her own change purse might be empty, living a life I wouldn't choose for me or for her.

And so, I call her and say, "Today I saw women out walking with their arms linked and laughing and it made me think of all the things a woman can do in this life when she's not focused on finding a man." I also say, "I'm starting to sleep better here" and "My French is coming back and I'm eating lots of cheese and bread and walking all day." I say, "I have friends." She says, "Good for you, honey," in a voice I recognize. A voice that's very busy trying to drift away. A voice of boredom or of caution, I think mostly it's caution. A voice that doesn't know where it's meant to fit. "Good for you" is her bookmark, her placeholder. I'm speaking a language she doesn't want to learn. Good for you isn't good for me, or it is good for me but maybe it's not so good for her.

My mom supported this move to Europe on paper but not in practice. "Maybe just put it off until next year," was her response when it felt like nothing would line up. When the first place I booked in Italy took my money and then disappeared from the internet. I call my mom whenever I need advice. When Nathan couldn't decide what he wanted to do after high school and seemed stuck, and I was worried all the time, so worried. When Nick would be especially sweet and my breath would hitch in my throat when I watched him sleep, and I'd think, *I can't leave him.* I'd call my mom like I always did, looking for the advice I always wanted and getting the advice she has given. *Wait. Don't go to school this year, just wait six months. Let's wait to go to Disney World for a year. Don't buy a car, don't write your book, don't apply for that new job. Wait.* She didn't tell me to wait out of spite. Maybe she told me to wait because she too has waited, and she wanted this to be the best true thing for us both. She wanted all the waiting to be right for us both, to work for us both. I think maybe sometimes she doesn't know how to not want us to be the same as each other. To want the same things, to drift through life making the same mistakes with the same results.

When I was in high school, I worked at a restaurant on the side of Highway 11 between Orillia and Gravenhurst called the Chalet. It served broasted chicken and bacon and eggs and good apple pies from scratch. My mom was the manager. She was a career waitress before she retired to move to California with my stepdad when Nathan was six years old. I'd call her Chalet years her Golden Age for sure. She had dozens of loyal regulars who liked her singular combination of sass and subservience, all entranced when she talked to them as though they were impish toddlers. "It's self-serve here guys. I'm not your slave," she'd say to the construction workers and retired golfers who hassled her for a refill of coffee when she was busy at another table. Or "You're a real prince among men, you know that, right?" She'd insult them and mock them even as she filled up their coffees and remembered every single thing they liked to eat without them having to say a word. Their eggs over easy, their bacon extra crispy. Marmalade not jam, milk not cream. She loved waking up to go to work for 6:00 a.m., loved filling up the salt and pepper shakers and those silver napkin dispensers, and loved marrying the ketchup bottles and refilling them from the bag of Heinz in the cellar.

I started working there when I was seventeen and I think she hoped I would love it too. I did, in a way. I loved her there. Not like she was my mom, like she was a woman who was full of sunshine. We dressed exactly the same for work even though no one else did, navy shorts and white t-shirts and swinging ponytails in the summer. "You could be sisters," is the thing everyone said and says still. I liked waitressing a little but I wanted more, always more. I wanted to go to university, and she said it wasn't going to happen, there was no money.

I wanted to go for an English degree and my stepdad pointed out I might as well be going for a degree in basket weaving. School was a waste of time, but more than that, it wasn't something she knew how to want for me since she hadn't gone for long. Just six weeks and then she found out she was pregnant with me and said goodbye forever. When I wanted to go to work on a cruise ship, she told me, "Oh my God, you watch too much TV, honey, you need to just get a regular job." When I graduated high school, I decided I wanted to go to Europe to be a nanny for a year and she said, "No. Who will I get to cover your shifts?" But for the first time, I said, *yes*. I dipped my toe into a new pool. It was hard for her then, losing me to Europe, but also losing the faintest idea of who she thought we were going to be together. Twin waitresses tag-team fighting with the kitchen manager when he shortchanged us on our sides of gravy and gossiping about the other waitresses when they didn't bother to refill the salad dressings at the end of their shift. When I left for Europe, she cried and said goodbye. A little bit to me, and a little bit to us.

I lived in Switzerland for a year and spent much of it trying to figure out who we were to each other. Not boys or friends or me, I thought about us. Me and my mom. Trying to write us as a movie that might make sense. But there was her version and my version, and I didn't know which one was fiction. In my version I was a little girl with a mother who was always in the other room. Always with adults at the kitchen table, my aunts and my nana and sometimes my grandpa, if she'd made him a Salisbury steak for dinner. I'd hide under the table so I could listen in on her stories about working as a bartender at a local hotel, the people she cut off from another whisky or another pint of Labatt's, and the waitresses who didn't know how to carry a tray or stop flirting with the customers. Under the table I waited to hear my name and I waited to be remembered and it never came. Not once, not that I remember.

I wanted her to touch me on my hair or my face or my back. Not because she needed me to move out of the way or to comfort me because I fell off my bike, a distracted pat on the back and her saying, "You're okay, you're okay." I wanted her to not think about touching me. I wanted it to be just the most natural thing for her to reach out and stroke my head. I wanted it to be so regular that I could shrug my head away and go, "Yuck, Mom!" and she'd laugh indulgently. One time this happened. I was sitting on the floor beside her and she was cross-legged and thirty years old and stunning, like an actress, wearing a bandana in her hair and a navy tank top and worn jeans. I was a kid with a bad haircut and baby-blue satin shorts and a red t-shirt that advertised Disco, leaning on her while she absentmindedly stroked my hair, her fingers cool and long and easy. I remember being terrified to move in case she realized what she was doing and stopped. Worried her hand would drop and she'd shift a hip away from me and I'd be alone. Always worried she'd notice me and then decide to stop noticing me.

She doesn't remember this. Instead, she remembers a little girl who laughed all the time and slept in a warm bed and had more clothes than she would have been able to imagine as one of eight children. When she was a girl, her coat was always wrong and her uniform tights were pink, not white like the other girls.

My thing is true and her thing is true. And our two true things keep changing on me. It's true that she can say things that make me blush with shame, has said things. About my weight, about my silliness, about my below-average singing voice. Jokes, always jokes. But the blush comes just the same.

It's also true that she saved me. Many times over. When I was married and sick and afraid. She came to rescue me with her purse bouncing on her hip and taking the stairs two at a time to bring me to her home to feed me and love me. She saved me when I was raising the boys. Once it was Callum's birthday and I had no money. I couldn't breathe for how many times this had happened already. I called her hyperventilating, to do I don't know what in California, and she said, "Check your cookie jar on the top of the fridge." She'd left a cheque for $200 the last time she visited because she knew I'd need it.

I loved her then. I love her now. I love her every time I try to solve the mystery of what our real love story might be. It's the only story in my life that matters sometimes. Like she's the only problem I have to solve. So much of what we've done is the same: the bad choices in men, the children, the years of waitressing. Single moms only twenty years apart, young and too dumb to be afraid. Skating along the edge of the pond of poverty and sometimes slipping beneath the surface.

My mom is slipping away from me on the phone on a Sunday in Avignon. She's bored or thinking about cleaning her bathroom. Maybe thinking about heading to Curves for thirty minutes, and then coming home to cook a marinated Greek chicken for dinner for my stepdad. I feel panicked. I want to pull her back into my *now*, but instead we slip into our *before*. We only know how to talk to each other in the past tense. *Do you remember when?* And these are never the same, we almost never *remember when* the same way, except for when we do.

I sit with my feet propped up on the white ledge of my window, picking at a piece of roast chicken from the night before. My legs feel good, hot and sore from cycling along back roads in the actual south of France. I let it go for a minute, the story of us. I go ahead and talk about *before*. Talk about when I found out I was pregnant for the first time. About how she tried to be happy for me then. How she tried not to think of what people would think because she was so goddamn tired of what people thought, but it was too late for her. She did say to me, "You don't have to get married, you know," and this was good advice. In that moment she was the truth-teller, the salmon swimming against the stream who didn't push her daughter to get married, the way she was pushed so hard. She was pushed so hard to fix things because of me and after me. She was thinking of her life all those years ago and thinking of how she just wanted to be a mom more than anything, but marriage was her admission price. Any marriage. I've never been forced to pay the price, not like her.

We talk about Callum then, her precious grandson. My precious boy. With him there will always be real happiness we can share. Now she comes back to me on the phone. She doesn't slip away and I don't try to force her to want everything I want. This is what I'm doing with that little change purse of happiness. I want to fill it with foreign currency, and she's hoping to just use the money she already has.

I stop then, stop trying to convert her. And she is full of sunshine.

The Most Naked Thing

So, I'm sitting in this bistro trying out an experiment that's just eating dinner alone. This probably seems like not so much of a big deal except to every woman I've talked to. It's a very big deal. Liza calls dinner out alone "the most naked thing" and she's right, normally it's terrible. Breakfast is fine and so is lunch, but dinner means you're really alone. I'm in this place that's like a French diner from the fifties and they're famous for their toast. The floors are faded black and white, the tables are small and round with little tablecloths. Big windows overlook a square where university kids are hanging out pretending to be bored in their best nonchalant clothes. I order a giant piece of toast with three melted cheeses and some pear, plus a salad. The waiter is young and thin, the kind of thin where you can tell he doesn't like being thin. He's bent double with the insecurity of it. But his smile is easy, so maybe I'm wrong about this. He's the one to tell me to try the toast and I know he wants me to like it. Beside my table, a young German couple smiles at me and orders in English. She's blonde and tentative and so is he. They order a dark-chocolate-and-hazelnut tart to share with coffees. I watch the waiter take his time to put equal amounts of real whipped cream on either side of the tart, so they'll have one thing that isn't shared between them. Whipped cream all around. Another man in a scarf and a sweater sits eating a salad at a table and reading a book, sort of like me. I think, *We're both happy for each other.*

We're all getting along nicely and separately and I'm thinking I might be sort of in love with my corner and my wine and my meal and my open journal. I'm thinking that eating alone doesn't feel lonely at all. I'm so relaxed that I'm already starting to wonder if I should order the lemon tart with a coffee and stay a while, we all feel so nice together. Then three Americans arrive and they have to own all the air in the room.

Everyone sort of slumps and shifts to make room for their energy but it's okay, they're going to take all the space anyhow. They are two older women and one older man, and I'm sorry to tell you, I know the older man. I know only four people in France, and he's one of them. He's probably nice when he's not working at his job of making sure everyone knows he's American. I want to tell him he could maybe take the day off because everyone can tell immediately.

The two women visit all the tables to see which one is the best. For a minute I'm worried mine will be the best and they'll take it, so I don't look up. They pick the table close to me and loudly order as many dessert items as they can muster. The man calls me over and says, "Don't be shy, you can sit with us," like this is a thing I want. I join them because we're all being clichés of our countries and I don't know how to stop being Canadian. I look longingly at my little table but there's no going back.

I sit there for exactly twenty-seven minutes. I learn that they're the best at everything they've ever done and I don't know what to say when they pause for me to agree. One lady is the best artist with the best haircut and the most knowledge of Avignon since she's lived here forever, but she doesn't speak French. The other lady knows everything about Canada because she went to Vermont for two weeks. She tells me we're not as great as we think because of that bad mayor of Toronto. I tell her he's dead and she says, "Still, I've been to Toronto, it's nothing special." I think, *Maybe we're in a film of American clichés*, and then I see they don't know they're a cliché, so I order my lemon tart to go. My new waiter friend and I share an eye roll at the counter. I tell him I'm Canadian so he knows I'm nice, and he says, "Yes, I thought so. Canadians are always so nice. I want to visit there someday." He doesn't charge me for my tart. Because, I guess, if you're going to be a cliché you should probably be a good one.

Mattresses Don't Bounce

Camili Books & Tea is about a five-minute walk from the studio. There you can buy second-hand books in English. It's a sweet store with a small garden courtyard out the back where I could write for hours perched under a tree if I wasn't so afraid of birds. Just like in Rome, the birds in Avignon are confident and well-fed by locals who give them their crusts of bread, their flight paths unhindered by my fear of one of them swiping the side of my head by the flap of a wing. I found this store because of another Facebook group of expats, the kind that's just meant for women.

Camili Books & Tea has a French-English conversation group that meets on Friday nights, and I join the very first Friday after I arrive — French- and English-speakers, mixing back and forth between the two languages so seamlessly. I feel like I've arrived at a party at 11:30 p.m. that was meant to end at midnight. There are students there too, a young American called Kevin who won't speak any English at all because he's attending the university in Avignon and wants to become fluent by summer. I watch him flower under the near-constant praise of two older French women who tell him his accent is charming, his vocabulary is incredible and his drive impressive. He stirs his sugar into his coffee one packet at a time until it's a syrup. I watch him want to please everyone, with his deep, confident American laugh when he understands a joke — that's a relief, he's so relieved. He's just a boy, like my boys. Sitting beside him, I want to collect up his sugar packets, and so I do. I wipe the granules off the table with the flat of my hand and he shifts a bit to let me clean up after him, a ritual. Sitting beside him, I think of making grilled cheese for my boys as they sat at the kitchen table talking to me, the four bottom breads lined up with the four tops. The frying pan warming up. Soup on the stove. Their stories about friends and about after-school jobs and about teachers who just don't understand them falling on me like soft easy raindrops. Like 24-piece puzzles I could solve easily, like I did when they were little, puzzles they couldn't solve without me.

I ask Kevin quiet questions in English and he answers me under cover of louder conversations in English. He's covert, eyes darting left and right over his cup of syrupy coffee, unwilling to speak his native tongue in front of the others. He answers in short spurts: from California, two parents, two siblings, wanted to live in France. He doesn't like Trump, not that I ask, but answering for Trump is something Americans are expected to do in Europe, whether they like to or not. I met a couple on a train in Orvieto who apologized to me for Trump and said, "We didn't vote for him, that's for goddamn sure." They flirted with the idea of moving to Canada. Kevin says something similar, that his parents considered moving to Canada but were concerned about the taxes. And this reminds me that sometimes Americans think moving to Canada is as easy as ordering replacement headphones from Amazon. Kevin doesn't want to live in Canada, and I can see he doesn't want me to mother him either. I feel a bit soft-eyed, clearing away his saucer and his sugar packets, trying not to smooth down his collar that's turned a bit in the back. He doesn't look relieved at my attention. He looks uncomfortable. He wants to have a conversation like a man, and I'm a stranger who seems to want him to take part in some sort of perverse role-playing game.

I'm not his mother. He's not my son.

At Camili, I also meet Muriel, a French psychologist with a chic angled bob and terrific red rectangle glasses. Her English is outstanding, but even better, she's the sort of person who corrects my French in a way that is natural, like she's reminding me of a little item on my grocery list I've forgotten. *You wanted the orange-rind marmalade, remember?* Muriel and I find seats close to an older American, also from California. Dennis has been living in Avignon for twenty-two years but he doesn't speak French. "Oh, I can get by fine, it's not that hard," he tells us. He likes the culture and the food but not the language. When Dennis hears me talking about the second-hand bike I just bought, he asks me where I'm going to go riding. I've never been able to read maps so I'm looking for a guide, and Dennis says, "Oh, you're one of those women who thinks because you're beautiful, people will just do all the work for you." I'm offended and irritated but pleased too because that was my training. Dennis tells me to meet him at Hôtel d'Europe on Sunday so he can take me out for a ride and show me the real sites. I'm reminded faintly of Tim from Italy, a confident traveller who decided that he knew best how to see a thing. A check-the-box kind of man. I tell him I won't be there, and he says I will, and I decide we'll have to wait and see who's right. Probably me.

There are other people at the conversation group too. An American who insists she's Parisian and tells me she heard Canada was so boring and provincial, and I think, *I hate your stupid glasses.* A young man with a stutter who doesn't speak French or English from what I can tell, just holds a plastic shopping bag on his lap and drinks tea with his head bowed, his leg shaking. A trio of older men who sit away from us all and talk into the middle of the table together. No one suits me like Muriel, and so I whisper to her, "Want to get a drink after?" and she instantly says yes. We leave as the group starts to disperse in that easy way of an evening mostly well spent. People are making plans to see each other that probably won't happen, everyone knowing it won't happen, but the concept of a different life is thrilling nonetheless. A woman from Norway who's recently moved to Arles invites the two older French women who so love young Kevin to her apartment for tea and they say yes. They coil scarves around their necks with their fingers spread wide in exactly the same way. A precise, elegant movement. Casual and effortless. They call to mind a woman I saw riding her bike to work that morning as I walked around the ramparts. Tall on her bicycle in a leather mini skirt and high heels, a short coat and a big blanket scarf and a cigarette between her fingers. When her skirt hitched up a little, she put her cigarette between her teeth while she adjusted it without breaking stride. A perfectly French moment.

Muriel and I walk over to a late-night bistro in Place Pie, a little spot that looks out over the town square with a heated cobblestone patio and soft blankets slung on the backs of chairs for extra warmth. We talk about her boss and her partner, about my Nick and my work. Maybe it's because she's a therapist and is very good at eye contact, but all of a sudden I'm telling her everything about us. About how he wants me to live with him when I go back to Canada and I don't think I can do it. I tell her about his mess and his piles.

Nick has these piles, you see, that follow him wherever he sits. A pill bottle full of loose change and nail clippers. A plastic container that was once used for ice cream but now holds nuts and bolts. Some receipts he swears he'll need when he does his taxes but will just sit on the island in his kitchen until the end of time. His day planner, bought by me, inscribed *To the Nicktator* that made him laugh and laugh. I tried living with Nick, I tell her — like we'd known each other for thirty years, in the way of new people who might not see each other again. She tells me it's time for me to move in with him. Just like that, with her half glass of wine and her blanket around her shoulders. Decisively, like it's one of those things I should already know. She tells me like we've had six sessions of therapy and it's finally time for her to share her conclusion. She doesn't know the history.

She doesn't know about the time I tried to live with Nick and Jack and Nathan after Callum and Ben moved out. I don't tell Muriel that living with Nick was like I'd put on a movie that no one wanted to watch but me. How he didn't understand that he doesn't understand kids. How Nathan and I fought so bad when I drove him to school some mornings that I went back to bed for an entire day, and I thought I lost the person I was supposed to be to him forever. How Jack stopped making eye contact with me and Ben spent a summer sleeping in a tent outside Nick's cabin because the promised renovations never happened. There was no room for him. There was no room for us. How Callum spent a summer lightly homeless because there was no bed for my twenty-one-year-old son in my new home. How after all this, after my kids kept their mouths shut and tried to fit themselves into this new life, Nick told me he thought I should move out until my kids were grown because of the mess of us all. He didn't say this, of course. He said, "I think I shouldn't be selfish and I should let you move out until the boys are grown."

Muriel doesn't know the me I was back then. I wasn't this happy person who could afford two glasses of wine and half a cheese board like it was no big deal. Then, I was working three part-time jobs that didn't amount to one full-time job. I was behind on so many bills I stopped opening my mail. And when Nick asked me to leave, I lay in bed that night staring at the window seat in our shared bedroom with the second-hand pillows in various floral prints I'd bought. I thought I'd never have what I want. That I'd never have a man and children to love at the same time. Muriel doesn't know about the parts of me that broke away from Nick when my boys and I drove away in a caravan of second-hand cars full of my second-hand wares from his log cabin one Saturday. The log cabin where I had painted the floor of the porch and where I arranged the kitchen cupboards just so and where I hung my sheets on the clothesline and listened to the crickets at night. She doesn't know I loved that cabin like a person. She doesn't know that when we drove away from the cabin, I watched my bed topple out of the cab of a friend's truck and bounce along the road. Everyone there, my kids and my friends, all laughed and grabbed the mattress and tied it down. It was a real comedy of errors, so typical of me and my wrongness. I didn't help tie it down. I couldn't move from behind the steering wheel. I just sat there gripping and gripping.

Only Nathan knew. When my boys were picking out their rooms in my new rented house, getting ready to order pizza and play video games, and pretending that six months or so had never happened, the only person who saw how I was feeling that day was Nathan. And he said to me in my car when we were alone, "This is a sad day for you, I know. It's okay if you want to cry. I won't tell anyone." Muriel doesn't know I cried so hard then, but it was relief. Here was a very good man I was creating. My Nathan. I was coming back to him.

I only tell Muriel about the deep love I feel for Nick. The painting over of patched-up walls that I try not to notice any longer. She only hears about a man who is supportive and kind, who backs me in my adventures. Who sends me crossword puzzles across the ocean addressed to "The" Jen McGuire and looks up every place I visit on Google Street View to find the good cafés and plays me songs on the telephone.

I don't think I can ever go back to the cabin and try to call it home. No matter what. Even though it's the place where we buried my dog, Lily, in November. Nick is the one who drove me to the vet and we both sobbed as we said goodbye to her, so old and faithful and as good as any dog ever. Nick is the one who dug her grave with me. The cabin is where my boys played music around the fire and helped build a screened-in porch. Where I've hosted countless pizza nights and Christmas parties and dinners. I'm afraid to love it again. Afraid to be the woman watching her double bed bounce under the wheels of an oncoming truck and split at the seam knowing she won't be getting a new bed ever, no matter what. Knowing she isn't that sort of person.

I tell Muriel I'll think about it. And she smiles, her work done.

Squeamish about Role-Playing

I had a crush on my first landlord after I left my husband, a man called Jackson, who was responsible for making sure my kitchen appliances were in good working order and wore a leather jacket from Danier in all weather. He was my age, which was just thirty at the time, but he was thirty without four small children, so he felt very young to me. One time I invited him over, pretending my stove was broken by unplugging it from the back. I wore a smocked red top with bootcut jeans and brushed my hair many, many times. Jackson came in with a lot of gel in his hair and wearing cologne. We talked about people we might have in common. Matt Sheldon from my eighth-grade class, apparently working at the nuclear plant and making some serious coin, I was told. Jackson told me a variety of tales that all ended in people making a lot of coin, and I felt like a teenager forced to sit at the kids' table. Too old and too changed and too tired to listen. He stopped being a crush.

After Jackson came two teachers at the elementary school who were faithful crushes for several years. Both married and both kind and both exactly the right amount of good-looking for me. Handsome without being dazzling. One was Callum's grade-three teacher when we first moved to town. The sort of teacher who made boys who liked school sit up taller because there he stood, an example that smart guys are cool sometimes. The kids thought he was funny because he laughed at their jokes in the way where they could tell he liked them and wasn't just faking it. Kids are like anyone else. They know when you're faking it. The other was the same, a big Tom Selleck of a man who sang joyously along during Christmas assemblies. His low voice booming through "Santa Claus Is Coming to Town" as he tapped his foot and bobbed his head. His voice always gentle, his smile always wry.

These crushes were normal for a woman in her thirties I thought. I guessed. I've decided. They were Hallmark movie fantasies. Men I liked for me and I liked for my kids. I liked them because I never had to worry about them liking me back. I liked to carry little fantasies of them around with me during my daily walks, highly detailed stories where I could whittle my potential outfits down to the shoe brand, but any passion was benign. My stories always included some soup in a slow cooker waiting for our return from a hike where I'd wear a thick braid and a flannel shirt. Maybe a man's sweater if that man was the Tom Selleck–type teacher because he was bigger than me. My fantasies included meals together and walks and hand-holding. Curling up on the sofa for a movie under a blanket. Separate blankets even, on either side of the sofa. These fantasies never got past the second date.

Other fantasies made it past the second date but not far. There was a café in Owen Sound called the Bean Cellar where a person could get a very good grilled meatloaf sandwich and find men to think about. I used to go there sometimes when I didn't have to work and the kids were in school. I'd go there and I'd bring my journals and enough money for two coffees and a piece of banana bread or a glass of water and a meatloaf sandwich. I'd make small talk with the men who came in. Some local musicians and writers or that single father with distracted eyes who brought his toddler in for some broccoli soup. My preferred spot was in a deep armchair near the front door. The kind where I could cross my legs but couldn't get out of it elegantly, especially if anyone was watching. The see-saw motion, the manoeuvring to climb out of the chair's depths. Around me there were other armchairs filled up with these men who filled me up with third-date fantasies. Men with serious beards and ironic t-shirts and cargo pants whose pockets were full of things like handkerchiefs and promotional artwork they'd scribbled for their next self-produced CD. Men who knew all the same pop culture references I knew, saying things like "Prestige Worldwide," like it was a secret joke. But if there had been a buzzer around, I could have buzzed in and said, "What is *Step Brothers*?" Men who gave guitar lessons to kids like mine and called them "cool dudes" and seemed to mean it. Here were the men who brought me out of my fugue state, where I hadn't thought of my body in years. Here were the men who made me want to have the sort of body they would consider for a Saturday night of sex and a Sunday morning of coffee and bacon and eggs before the boys came home and then they would, of course, have to be gone.

My mother told me when I left my husband that he was probably my last kick at the can, and boy was I furious. Of course, men would still want me, four sons or not. I was wrong and I was right. Some men still wanted me, but I didn't want them. The man who was a regular at Joe Tomato's, who invited me for breakfast and ate peanut butter toast that sat congealed in the sides of his mouth while he told me things I didn't care about. The seventy-year-old real estate developer who told me he could show me a good time "if you're not squeamish about role-playing." Mostly though I couldn't be bothered. Mostly romantic period dramas and my new vibrator were enough for me. Safer than the alternatives. Probably more fun too.

When I worked at a clothing store at the mall there was a woman called Liz who wasn't squeamish about role-playing. She was a single mom like me and a bit round like me. Liz was the kind of girl who actually loved the khaki pants and sweatshirts with kittens coquettishly hiding in flowers we were required to wear. The laces of her sneakers always tied in neat little bows, her lunch bag packed with a turkey sandwich with mayo and some rice cakes and an apple. She folded jeans in tidy piles from size 2 to size 14 so that the cuffs were always folded on the inside, arranged pastel plaid blouses with coordinating scoop-neck t-shirts layered underneath them on hangers. Liz's dream was to become the assistant manager. But also, she spent every second weekend in Toronto wearing leather corsets and dog collars and having sex with much older men. She told me this once when we were out for a drink after work, maybe about three months into working together. She told me about this because she knew I was a single mom too and might appreciate the extra work if I wanted to come along. "It's not so bad," she said while stirring her tequila sunrise. "The man who set me up takes care of everything. He sends me bus fare to get to Toronto then picks me up from the station and brings me to one of those nicer hotels, you know the kind where you get to have a living room *and* a bedroom?" (I knew the kind.) "He orders the outfits for me and leaves them in a box at the hotel and I just wear whatever he orders.

Plus I get to keep them after if I want." I asked her to describe the outfits. "Mostly they're these corset things that either lace up or zip up that you can keep on during sex because there's no crotch in them. Sometimes they like me to wear these big, tall heels so I can step on them a bit, but I think that's going to stop because I never step hard enough. I'm always worried I might really hurt one of them and then I'll be in trouble. Then they like me to wear a mask sometimes, or maybe just this necklace that has a little thing attached like a leash or whatever." Liz went on to tell me that the men were pretty old and sometimes they couldn't have sex, they just touched her a lot. She got paid no matter what, even if they couldn't have sex, and one of the best parts was that they all liked to eat a big steak dinner together at the end. "I order whatever steak I want. I don't even look at the prices." I told Liz I probably wasn't interested but it sounded like a great opportunity.

At first, I felt quite sorry for Liz. She was a sweet woman who baked cakes for extra money and kept her house tidy and had her kids' permission slips tacked to a corkboard in her kitchen. She never went to Toronto when her kids were home for the weekend. I felt sorry for her but, also, I thought maybe she was making an empowered decision, taking ownership of her sexuality in a way I wasn't mature enough to fully comprehend.

Now I think Liz was just a single mom who was damaged like we all are. A woman whose self-esteem had taken a battering. A woman who didn't think men would want her and didn't know how to deal with a world where men might not want her and thought she found a way to change the story, but it wasn't really her story at all. I watched Liz change over the months after she told me about her weekends in Toronto. In April we were working a rainy shift together and she told me about how the hotel room had changed to the regular kind and she had to pay her own way to Toronto. How the men didn't always want her to stay and eat steak with them, and one time she was given money to order pizza in her own hotel room after a night because "some of the men got a little out of hand." I saw her bruises, black-and-purple fingerprints on her throat under the turtleneck she wore adorned with a tiny smiling snowman. Her kids started to spend more time with her mom at her house in the country, but Liz kept going to Toronto. She didn't know how not to go to Toronto on the four-hour bus ride. Hoping to feel like a girl in a corset who was powerful and desirable and looking forward to her sixteen-ounce T-bone, price upon request. Eventually I quit my job and didn't see much of Liz, but I wondered sometimes. I wondered about her a lot of the time.

My crushes never moved beyond crushes. The married teachers stayed married and I wouldn't have wanted them to become single. The landlord eventually sent me a bill for the carpets in the rec room that were destroyed by the dog I wasn't supposed to have. The musicians sold me their CDs at full price. I stayed single for almost the entirety of ten years. I was just so goddamn afraid.

My Size 12 Ass

About five years ago, I lost 40 pounds or 50 pounds or 100 pounds depending on how fat you thought I was before I lost the weight. I didn't weigh myself in the beginning and so I couldn't weigh myself at the end. I gave up weighing myself after I joined Weight Watchers when I was a twenty-four-year-old mother of two who clocked in at 235 pounds. My Aunt Brenda and I joined it together during the big January sale when Ben was four months old and Callum was two years old. Meetings were held at the United Church around the corner from her house. There was no big gimmick in those days, no special apps or points system, just folding chairs and women looking flushed while they got weighed, for good reasons or bad reasons, depending. At the meetings we always talked about food, visualizing a Cadbury Creme Egg melting in the sun or thinking about being forced to drink a cup of chicken fat to stop us from craving the things we ate to make us happy. Some women there wore shirts that boasted they'd been proud members of Weight Watchers for five years or ten years or twenty years, shirts that were tight and poorly made with the lettering chipping away from too many washes. One of these women, an older lady in her seventies wearing elastic waist jeans and white orthopaedic sneakers, gave me this helpful tip during a meeting, "Sometimes if I can't wait until the next morning to eat, I just stay up until midnight and have a snack. Cereal or maybe just a handful of bacon bits since they're not very many points. That way I can count those calories for the next day, see?"

I didn't lose weight on Weight Watchers or if I did lose five pounds it came back the next month. My aunt and I both quit because all that talk about food made us hungry and we ended up at Dairy Queen after for a treat, a Reese's Peanut Butter Cup blizzard and a chocolate-dipped cone. I tried all sorts of tricks, like most women. I tried intermittent fasting. I'd eat two days' worth of food between 11:00 a.m. and 7:00 p.m. and then think about eating for the rest of the night. I tried my nana's trick of eating half of whatever I planned on eating. "Just eat one piece of toast instead of two, or half a cup of cottage cheese with peaches instead of a whole cup." I tried the juice fast, several versions of high-protein and low-carb and gluten-free diets, veganism and vegetarianism. I obsessed over food and danced in my living room with both Jane Fonda and Richard Simmons. I did step class with Susan Powter and joined aquafit classes at the gym and worked out with exercise balls and did Pilates and belly dancing and spin classes. I cycled marathons on stationary bikes. I don't know what I weighed through all that but I do know I really hated myself a whole lot all the time. I hated my calves for not fitting into knee-high boots and I hated all the women who could zip themselves into them so carelessly, without having to think about it at all. I hated my arms and my stomach and my ass and my breasts, even if I wore low-cut tops to show off my cleavage so that no one would look at the rest of me. I hated going out with friends for a night where they'd compliment me on whatever long flowing top and leggings combo I wore, but they didn't mean it. I hated shopping in plus size stores and I hated being so vapid that I cared about those kinds of things.

When I did finally lose a bit of weight and kept it off, I didn't do it because of all the things I hated about myself. I didn't do it for my kids. They didn't care. All the things I hated about myself were invisible to them and I guess maybe that was how I gained weight in the first place. At the beach no one looked at me in my bathing suit because I was with four kids, and I'll tell you, this was bliss. I wanted it to be bliss. I told myself it was empowering to be invisible and it was and, of course, it wasn't. I didn't lose weight to find a man either. I went on some dates and had some sex and felt fine, just fine most of the time. Extended calf boots were invented and I found a pair on sale at Addition Elle. There was a body-positivity revolution happening in the world right around then. It gave me enough of a boost to feel just slightly more confident, and with that confidence I met a man or two. Sure, if a man didn't love me then I assumed it was because I was fat. I dated a man before Nick I really loved. Someone I thought I could build a life with, a fellow writer and a single dad who was good at being a single dad. A movie person. We dated in secret as per his wishes. No one in our small town knew. When he emailed me that he had met someone, I knew she'd be thin and I was right. For six months my head was fuzzy and confused. Full of him and full of the nice life I thought we could have together and full of his new girlfriend's long-legged, lanky yoga body. Still, I didn't lose weight for him. I lost weight because of diabetes. I didn't want diabetes.

It's a big trend in my family, getting diabetes. That and drinking Diet Coke and smoking and eating Kentucky Fried

Chicken with the moist bread if you can find a place that's still selling moist bread. My nana started the diabetes fad in our family; she had it at least my entire life. When I was a kid, I thought having diabetes meant you got to keep Laura Secord chocolates under your bed and have cans of pop in the fridge no one else was allowed to touch. I thought diabetes meant you could take naps whenever you wanted, middle of the morning or early evening or during dinner if you didn't like what was being served. I thought diabetes meant you were allowed to carry plastic bags full of jujubes in your purse and never have to share them, not even with your grandchildren. My nana made diabetes seem like a pretty great way to live your life, so I didn't worry about it much as a kid. We lived with my grandparents most of my childhood, until I was thirteen and my mom met my stepdad, so I grew up with diabetes. This was the house where all my grandparents' eight kids visited, at least two a weekend it seemed. Some of them had diabetes and some didn't, but they all ate the same. Late-night pizzas with extra green olives from Pizza Delight. Bologna wrapped around a slice of cheddar cheese and dipped in mustard while they played cards at the table. Bags of Ruffles plain chips with French onion dip on the side. Chilled mint Oreo cookies on a shelf in the fridge that wasn't for the children. This was the theme of the snacks, *not for children*.

Diabetes was a problem in our house only when my nana decided to shoot herself up with insulin in the living room while my brothers and cousins and I watched Saturday-morning cartoons. There she'd sit with a handful of her bare belly, absent-mindedly jabbing herself. A cigarette waiting in the ashtray beside her. If any of us turned to look at what she was doing she'd say, "What? Do you have a problem with this?" So we learned to stare at the screen real hard until she was gone. I guess you could say stepping on insulin needles was also a problem, but we might have been asking for it. As kids, everyone knew the best treats in the house were under Nana's bed. Boxes of chocolates and, as we got older, historical romances where people had sex and made it sound sexy. Coloured stockings in lime greens and pinks we could use during dress-up and brimmed hats and costume jewellery mixed in with the rest of the detritus kicked under there. To get to these treats, we'd take turns sneaking into her room when she was out shopping with our moms for the afternoon. This meant running the gauntlet: stepping on old pop-can tabs and forgotten insulin needles hidden under books that would poke into your toes, sometimes getting stuck. It was worth it for the chocolates.

Diabetes was nothing as a kid, but as a woman in my forties, I had a friend who lost a toe to it. I didn't want to lose my toes and so I decided I'd lose a few pounds. Not a lot, I warned everyone when I thought they looked too excited, just a few pounds. I decided to take it easy. I decided to walk in the mornings with my friend Marcella, at first a five-kilometre walk through town, with one hill, and then we added another hill and another. The first time I climbed a hill I coughed and coughed like I'd never take a full breath again, but I kept going because I was getting happier. Marcella told me, "If I didn't go for walks, I'd be so depressed I'd fucking kill myself." Looking good was sort of a by-product for her and after a while it was for me too. We walked and gossiped our way all over town no matter the weather, climbing through snow so high we couldn't feel our knees at the end or sliding on our butts down a hill so icy we couldn't get a grip. From there I started playing pickleball with a group of old guys at the YMCA. I joined some outdoor yoga classes, one where I watched the sun rise over Georgian Bay and tried to calm my brain enough to meditate. I drank some green shakes and ate a little better. I tried to drink water but forgot a lot. And I lost weight.

I didn't lose the kind of weight where I'd become the heroine at the end of a movie. I went from wearing stretchy clothes in a size 18 to regular clothes in a size 12, however many pounds that might have been. I stayed the size of a person who could be called fat by people who do things like that when they're mad about something else. The end of my journey is likely someone else's beginning. There are people in my life now who still say things like, "You're so confident for a woman of your size." I've had men say, "I like a curvy woman, gives me something to hold on to" unprompted. Obviously unprompted. Mostly people are proud of me, prouder than they've been of anything else I've ever done in my life. Proud of my new cheekbones that poke out a little, proud of my ass that feels less obscene than the original. My sons tried not to say anything until I told them to say something and then they were proud. So proud. "I can lift you," Ben told me when he hugged me. He said it like it never occurred to him to care if he could lift me. A few friends asked me what I did but I didn't know what to say. I said that I'd write a diet book called "Ish" because I ate healthy-ish and exercised-ish. This wasn't what anyone wanted to hear.

The thing is, so far, I don't have diabetes. I can wear knee-high boots if they're pretty stretchy. I can buy underwear in a size large and order a dessert without blushing. I can walk around all day without anyone doing a double take, without anyone looking sad for me because of my hips.

By the time I arrived in Avignon, I'd been this size for about four years or so but there were still days when I turned back into the girl from before. The bigger girl who had to be funnier and better and more if she wanted to get through the day. Those days were getting further apart but still she came in the worst of her forms. When I was bigger, I was mostly joyful and sometimes wretched, but when I turned back into that girl sometimes, only the wretched version came out. The one who would stand in front of the bathroom mirror in speechless horror, real actual horror. Whose body felt like it was tattooed with all my shameful appetites — "butter" across my belly and "cheese" written out on my cheeks where all the world could see it. All the Chinese takeout, all the pizza and tacos and big pancake breakfasts that had brought me down so low, curling out of my skin like body hair I couldn't shave away. These visits never included any of the happiness I got from those meals, opening up the Chinese takeout with the boys, with Callum in the other room setting up the *Lord of the Rings* extended edition as the rest of us doled out our noodles and our beef and broccoli and our spring rolls. We'd sit cross-legged around our big coffee table eating and talking and shushing if the dialogue got real good. Warm cinnamon rolls on Christmas morning in our matching pyjamas, stockings in our laps full of Dollar Store toys and anticipation. Happy with our full bellies, full fridge, full of each other.

When my old self visits me, none of this comes back with her, it's just loneliness and darkness and hatred. And flesh that metastasizes no matter what I do. In dreams, I turn back into her, and my jeans won't button and my bras won't fit, and there's nothing I can do. No walking or biking, no swimming or yoga, nothing. In my dreams, I'm still the girl who went to the movies with friends and couldn't pay attention because I was thinking about my waist fat touching their arms or my thighs spreading out to their thigh space, and they wouldn't want to say anything, they'd shift away discreetly, but we all knew. We always knew I didn't fit. In my jeans or in my seat or in a kayak.

This girl always came back. She'd come back because the new version was just a visitor. Until she just didn't anymore.

She stopped coming back little by little in Avignon. Here I feel sexy, I'll tell you this, sexy in a way where I don't need a man to want me or a woman to be jealous of me. Every day I wake up and make myself a coffee to drink by my window in a patch of sun. I ride my bike or go for a walk or visit the market two streets away and practise my French (which, I admit, is getting quite good). The trick is to open with an apology about my broken French just in case. I'll say to the man with the really good roast chicken at Les Halles, "I'm trying my best, you know how it is." And he'll compliment me, smile at me. Smile at me like I'm really just a lot of fun. This is the change for me in France. I'm starting to feel like a lot of fun even when I'm just by myself. I'm starting to like being by myself. Really looking forward to it, like I have to make plans with myself and get dressed up and everything.

One sunny day when I'm not working, I ride my bike across the bridge to Villeneuve-lès-Avignon for lunch in the square, and even though pigeons are everywhere, I take my time. There are about five or six restaurants all around the square and it's my job as the customer to sit outside in the sunshine and decide which restaurant to choose. Don't worry, you can't make a bad choice. I choose a place that makes me a salad with a tiny baked potato stuffed with some sort of buttery chive-cheese combination and the most delicious lemony vinaigrette I've ever tasted. I drink two glasses of wine and eat a basket of bread and have to turn down dessert twice because I'm too full. The waiter is disappointed in me, shakes his head and tells me I don't know what I'm missing. I take my coffee by the fountain where I left my bike propped and then ride all over for hours by myself, my Spotify playlist streaming songs, like "Into the Mystic" or the Milk Carton Kids playing "Monterey" in my ears. The roads are flat and wide, exactly the kind of roads where a person can take their time passing a jewel-green river so translucent the smooth stones on the bottom reflect the sun. Side roads are lined with olive trees and grapevines and old stucco farmhouses, vanilla cream with red shutters. I meet a dog and a man and a little child. I stop late in the afternoon for some sort of flourless chocolate cake thing at a café where two other women are filling up their bags with lemon tarts and brioche and wedges of quiche and flatbread topped with strong cheese and black olives. This is a day where I speak to nearly no one, and at the end, when I ride home and shower and my skin feels tight and warm from the sun, boy I feel sexy. To no one but me or to everyone, it doesn't matter.

In Avignon, I start to shop for myself. Not as a mom and not with an eye for a discount. Really shop for the body I've grown into or down to. I buy a good white t-shirt and a bright-red lipstick with red lip liner and a navy blazer. I stop worrying about my hair that hasn't been coloured and is now the colour of beer, all malt and wheat and too many different lengths. I don't worry, because that tight-skinned sunshine happiness has started to feel normal to me in France. When I talk to the boys, they hear it in my voice, and I'm not sure if they like it. "You sound like you're having more fun now," one says, while another says, "Huh, you almost sound like you could live there." I tell them of course I couldn't, but sure I looked at real estate, why not?

I look at real estate and imagine myself living in Avignon in an apartment much like Liza's, a place where I've started to spend quite a lot of my time. Liza's apartment is just above mine at the end of a spiral staircase, two floors of the kind of place where a woman could be very happy. Books and books and more books everywhere. A big kitchen and a comfy sofa with not one but two little patios, one off her bedroom, which was the closest thing to a boudoir I've ever seen. Liza is seventy and she's also fifteen and she's also forty-five. She's lit up from the inside, mischievous. She teases everyone, but mostly herself. She teases Pierre for being morose and me for being clumsy and Pierre's girlfriend, Jeannie, for feeling sorry for herself. When Liza speaks, she draws me in close and slaps me away at the same time, but the thing I love the most is when she links her arm through mine. When she pulls me along beside her. When she chases pigeons away by screaming, "Tuk, tuk, tuk!" at them and feels so sorry for me and my "handicap."

I've started to dress a little better in Avignon and it might be for Liza or it might be for me, I don't know. Like most French women, Liza wears three or four outfits only because she knows her colours well, always in jewel tones with a good scarf and a pink lipstick. Always with sensible shoes that look sharp but work well on cobblestones. I start to pay closer attention to my clothes because Liza always notices, always comments. So do her friends.

On a Wednesday, we go to Saint-Rémy-de-Provence together to shop at the market and have lunch at her friend Cathy's house afterwards. The town of Saint-Rémy is chic, smaller than Avignon by several thousand people but with a reputation for being moneyed and it shows. The market winds its way through the streets and the vendors sell only the best of everything. The most fragrant lilac sachets and the best soap and the softest tablecloths in the most discreet colours and the chewiest macarons and the strongest cheeses. It's sunny, and I'm wearing just regular jeans and a button-down shirt but I feel good. I think it's the red lipstick. Several times I'm stopped by a vendor who gives me a free curl of soap for my smile or a small bag of raspberry macarons for my eyes. Liza and Cathy show me how to find the best olives and where to go for the best cheese, which they taste while the vendor watches expectantly until one of them nods and says, "Yes, he is good this one." They buy 100 grams only and then 100 grams of about three or four others.

I think this is when the old me stops coming back for her terrible visits. When I stop thinking so much about my size 12 ass. When I pick every 100 grams of cheese I buy like it's the last piece of cheese I'll ever buy, and what's more, the people who sell it to me want me to eat, they need me to eat. They smile at me and flirt. And even when people aren't selling me food, flirting just feels very fun in France. Silly and kind and exactly what I need.

One night, out for drinks with a new friend, a young handsome man comes up to tell me he thinks I'm beautiful. He says he noticed me and just wanted to tell me. He asks if I have a boyfriend and I say yes. He touches his hand to his heart dramatically and says in French, "Too bad for me." He buys my wine and leaves. Leaves me to bask in his compliment until my friend slips her arm in mine and starts to croon an old torch song about Lola getting what she wants. We walk home just like that. And just like that I become the regular new me.

Lipstick Stain on the Train

Liza is throwing me a little going away party tonight, before I leave. It's Saturday and she decides we should all bring something to eat. I figure I'll bring the good chicken from the good-chicken guy at the market and extra wine. I plan to meet a friend at the market for a coffee and a little shopping, but things have been weird from the start this morning. Weirder than I've seen yet. The entire city is closed down to avoid a protest from the Yellow Vests, a political group that spends most Saturdays protesting the French government in general and President Macron specifically. Liza explains that the original driving force behind the creation of the Yellow Vests was the idea that regular working men, the people who wear safety vests to their jobs, are largely ignored by the elitist government. They're fighting for economic justice, particularly protesting the exorbitant costs of gas in France that makes it difficult to drive to larger centres to work.

Every weekend since its formation in November, there have been small protests by the Yellow Vests. They've been happening in Avignon and other parts of France. Certainly I've seen several, but they hadn't really registered with me on those other weekends. Usually, it was a big group of mostly men, who were mostly white, shouting things in unison I mostly couldn't understand. There've been a few deaths during the protests, and many people have been blinded by pepper spray when the police got involved. The protesters would shout and march, but by evening, they would just disappear. Muriel explained to me during an afternoon in Marseille that other right-wing groups had joined the Yellow Vests, men who are upset about the burgeoning feminist movement in France. She thinks they're behind a lot of the violence that has started cropping up recently. When I saw the Yellow Vests in the past, I avoided them. It was easy enough.

This time feels different right away. More dangerous. More violent. Now it's not up to me to decide whether I want to pay attention. It turns out there's been a call across the country for all members of the Yellow Vests and the people who support them to converge on Avignon for the biggest protest yet. When I walk over to the market the air feels charged, nervous. All the entrances are blocked by police vehicles and there's only one way in, through rue de la République by the train station. I'm stopped and yelled at by a policeman and even though my French is passable by this point, I can't understand a word he says. It's all angry sounds and pauses at the end of sentences, hands in the air, like, *Are you an idiot?*

Inside, everyone is being searched as they come into the market, whether they're in a car or walking or on a bike. People look nervous or wretched or just plain angry. Especially one middle-aged man in a leather jacket. He has grey skin and grey hair and wears an old grey sweatshirt and jeans that are supposed to be black but have faded. He's short like a lot of French men, but he doesn't seem to take his stature with a shrug like some I've met. Like it's an inside joke they think is mildly amusing. He seems to be taking his 5'6" height pretty personally. Near him, I recognize a transgender woman I've seen at least a dozen times before, buying her vegetables and pastries and living her life like the rest of us. When the man sees her in her light-pink trench and black ankle pants and sunglasses, quietly holding her bag of greens, he begins to shout things at her. Awful things. The kind of things that make her flush and stare real hard at the endives nestled on fake grass at the greengrocer. I've never heard anyone shout anything at anyone before that in Avignon, unless they were happy or trying to sell cheeses. For the first time, I see people look away, ashamed of themselves for not saying anything. The market is already closing its doors, quick and quiet, and to me it seems like there are small groups of women and men whispering together and looking around nervously.

I meet my friend at the market finally, and we hug and buy our things. I'm so desperate to leave I forget about getting a final croissant. Afterwards we part ways and I make an enormous deal insisting she text me when she gets home, like I'm taking care of her. She's coming to the little party at Liza's tonight and I think she should consider staying at my place all day, but she says no. I go for a walk inside the rampart walls to clear my head, to think about home and being away and how I'm inside this city being part of its history. Everywhere is hollowed out, even at the Palais des Papes where, the night before, I sat on the steps listening to a man singing "My Funny Valentine" a cappella with such emotion, with hundreds of people standing hushed, listening, and falling a little bit in love with each other for just a minute. Now, there's no one anywhere. Restaurants are closed. We're all told to go home and stay inside. Liza sends me a message to make sure I make it back to the studio.

When I get home, I find a man pissing on my windowsill, drunk and angry as a slap across the face. When I unlock my door, he walks over to me with his penis in his hand, still dripping with his own urine. I get in the house and lock the door behind me. He stands outside my window staring and I know he can't see me because of my blinds but I still feel like he can see me. He wears a yellow vest peeking out from under his sweater. He leaves after precisely four minutes.

It's especially sunny today, especially warm. The lilacs from the neighbour's trellis across the street are in bloom and thank God they smell strong and sweet. I pack my suitcase but it's too hard to get the tight rolling of my long-sleeved shirts right. All I can hear is chanting and shouting. Rue Thiers is barricaded, but just outside the barricaded walls the police are in riot gear and protesters are trying to get inside, trying to be heard. I guess they're just trying to be heard. Liza is upstairs safe; I know this because a cop comes to the front door and starts pounding on it with urgency, midafternoon. I hear her open the upstairs window, ask him what he wants. In his riot gear, his shoulders look like a cartoon drawing of shoulders, like he can't make it through the door he's so big. He tells her to come down, with an authoritative tone, not taking off his sunglasses. I open my door so he can see me standing there in my leggings and tank top, so he knows she isn't alone. She opens the door and asks him what's going on. He whispers in her ear and she bursts out laughing. She turns to me and says, "He has to make pee pee. Can you believe it?" He grimaces a little but tries to keep his face impassive. Liza tells him to go upstairs to use the washroom and indeed if any of his fellow officers need to make pee pee they can come over too.

Later that night, the party is subdued. Maybe because of my departure or maybe it's the protests. The next day Liza will drive me to the train station after I clean the studio (to save myself a €40 cleaning fee). I'm packed and ready for the morning and feel childishly robbed of a big special goodbye. Robbed by the Yellow Vests for certain. Robbed until Liza says to me, "You know when you came, I was supposed to get a €200 deposit from you?" We all laugh except Pierre's girlfriend, Jeannie, who's rented Liza's studio and paid her €200 deposit. I say, "I would have paid it. Why didn't you ask?" She shakes her head, bemused. Wearing a loose cashmere sweater with jeans without rips and perfectly combed hair. Then she shrugs and says, "It was like falling in love when I met you. Yes, I think it was like we fell in love." I think so too.

In the morning, I wake up early to go for a final climb up the stairs. I don't know what I expected to see after the protests yesterday, but it wasn't this. Young women and one man in a rainbow-coloured wig doing disco-themed yoga in the park to ABBA. Families feeding the swans and little girls in pastel-coloured pea coats with long dark hair. Boats travelling up and down the Rhone, along with mostly rowers, but a few canoes and such too. The cafés are open and there's no garbage on the street, no evidence that anything happened. The people look pleasantly bored in that singular French way again. When I ask Liza about this in the car, she tells me, "Yes, what do you expect? We have manifestations all the time you can't go around crying about it, can you?"

It turns out nobody was scared but me. That it was all a high drama, and nobody was hurt and nobody died. Most of the Yellow Vests apparently stayed for the rest of the afternoon to make a day of it in Avignon. The restaurants opened back up, it was fine. Some apparently ate at one of my favourite restaurants, Le Bistro Lyonnais, where the waiter is also the chef and the waitress is his wife. It's just three streets away from my studio. I've ridden my bike there so many times, and, the thing is, they don't give you a menu. They just say, "Duck or fish?" and then feed you course after course of delightful food for three hours until you're drunk and sated and stumbling home like a toddler who needs a nap. I would have liked to see him wagging his finger at the Yellow Vests in his chef's hat and coat. I would have liked for him to feed me again too.

Liza didn't cry about the protests, about a lost sunny afternoon. But she does cry when we say goodbye. So do I. We stand behind her Fiat with the trunk open, in our scarves and our jeans and our lipstick on our lips and I want to say to her how much she's changed me. How she taught me about being alone in a way no one else ever could. How she sort of saved me a little bit by bringing her lady energy into my life. How she showed me all that was brave and honest and a little bit mean and funny and, best of all, fun. I want to tell her I'll come back to Avignon, I'll always come back. I want to tell her that even though I didn't do anything of significance here, every day was significant. How seeing movies with her at Cinéma Utopia and eating cheesecake at La Mirande, where we took high tea in the lounge under the enormous skylight and told each other about our lives, how it was a sacred thing to me. I want to tell her so many things about the person I was when I was a girl and the person I became as a mom and how she helped me get those two girls married and how they are extraordinarily happy living together inside me all of a sudden. I want to tell her all the things I love about her, the way she curses in French and embraces the word *cunt* with relish. The sing-song lilt of her voice. Her brusque kindness, her hard slaps on the arm to get my attention. Instead, I say, "There's a bottle of wine for you in the fridge and you can eat the rest of my chocolate." She smiles and kisses my cheeks again. Her pink-orange lipstick stays there until Marseille. I didn't see it.

Even if I had, I'd never have wiped it away. Not for anything.

You Think Well of Yourself

I wanted to be a writer since I was a little girl of about eight and wrote a poem about dolphins that I thought was really quite good. I showed it to my grandfather and he said, "Don't quit your day job," and in that moment I thought I'd show everyone I could do it, even him. I wanted to be a marine biologist for a long time too after I visited Sea World as a child. Forcing dolphins to be my pets was all I wanted then, also living on boats and sleeping in my bathing suit and diving with sharks. This was what I wanted before I wanted to be a writer and even for a while after, until my science marks came back with frowns in the margins. Writing stayed with me though. Through high school, where I got slightly higher than average grades in English classes, and through the years, when my friends were all in university and I was having babies. When my life was always backwards, always running behind the bus to catch up and never quite making it. I would have given anything to call myself a writer then. Anything. I guess I thought it would be more fun.

These days, I know that telling people you're a writer is irritating to everyone. It's like saying you're a sailor because you know how to sail or a tennis player because you have a regular Saturday game. You're not supposed to just list the things you like to do as your job. It was easier when I was a bartender who wrote or a daycare worker who wrote or a person who baked lemon squares for the local bookstore who wrote. I didn't have to tell people that I was secretly a writer unless I really wanted them to know, which was always but now it's almost never. It almost never comes up, this bit about me being a writer, not unless Nick's in the room acting like my walking resumé. He tells people about every essay I've ever written and usually ends up with "*and* ... she wrote for Oprah." He says this like I was sitting in Oprah's back garden with her springer spaniels at my feet writing her an essay in long hand with a felt-tip pen, but the truth is *O, The Oprah Magazine* just picked up an article I wrote one time for their website. It might have even been an accident. I like to tell myself Gayle King might have read it.

If Nick isn't around, I don't bring the writer business into conversation unless asked point-blank what I do for a living. And since I don't have any other jobs to hide behind anymore, I tell them. I tell them I write for my local newspaper and sometimes do some freelance writing and write for a website too. Then the questions start. What do I write about? And for whom? And do I get paid? And all that. Mostly I try to get it over quick so people can get back to deciding if they're going to like me or not, and mostly people are happy to move on. Being a writer is an uncomfortable sort of job that can make people feel like they're being examined because they are. I'm examining them. All the time. At a café or a bar or a house party where everyone is drinking, of course, I'm watching. I like to hang out at parties where I'm not drinking anything because then I get to watch things crumble in thirty-minute shifts. It's nice to be able to nose into people's business without them noticing, so I don't bring up the writing thing unless I have to. Like at border control where you don't get to pick your questions and have to tell the truth.

I was lucky in Italy at passport control, they just asked how long I was staying and sent me on my way. In Marseille, the passport control officer didn't ask me anything, he just winked and waved me on.

In Belfast things are different straight away. The line is short, only about thirty people or so, but it takes forever, even with four officers in their plexiglass cubbies. When it's my turn, I'm met by a short grey-haired man with a ruddy complexion and a stamper clutched in his fist. He asks me why I'm coming to Belfast, how long I'll be staying, those sorts of regular questions. When he asks me what I do for a living, I say, "Writer" because I don't have a choice. It's on my tax return. He stops and frowns. "Well, what do you write?"

"Just for newspapers and stuff," I reply.

"A journalist like?"

"No, not like that. Just a columnist."

He waits. It isn't enough. I add, "Like a lifestyle columnist."

"Well? What do you write about?"

"Um, me. I just write about my life."

"And what do you do with your life?"

I give this some thought. It's a profound question, some might even say too profound for a quick stamp on a passport. Standing there, I realize I've contributed nothing to the world, really have nothing of merit to offer. Dejected I say, "Nothing really. I don't do much of anything." And I feel emptier than anything all of a sudden.

He stamps my passport without looking at me. "You think well of yourself now, don't you?" I don't, I promise. Growing up I wasn't allowed to think well of myself or get too big for my britches or walk around with my nose in the air or act like Sarah Bernhardt who was an actress with a bad reputation in my family. If I cried or complained or acted hurt when one of my aunts commented on my large breasts when I was just twelve years old at the dinner table on a Sunday, this was when I was acting like Sarah Bernhardt. Or getting too big for my britches. Or walking around with my nose in the air, take your pick. This man could be my uncle or my aunt or my mom or my grandpa. He could be anyone in my family taking the reins of my ego and giving them a good tug so I don't get ahead of myself. He could be sitting in the living room in Owen Sound with the rest of them, with their cigarettes and Tab and science fiction books facedown on end tables. Waiting for one of the kids like me to come in and start showing off, start bragging about a new trick on their bike or a picture they drew that they considered especially artistic. Waiting to remind them, remind me, that we didn't need to be thinking so well of ourselves.

I should be offended by this border control guard in Belfast but I'm not. Instead I am home.

Joseph Leo McGuire

Belfast smells like my grandpa. Like the fresh tar of his driveway, like the pipe he smoked sometimes when he was trying to lay off the cigarettes. Like the kettle on the stove that sat steeping on the back burner all day, that tangy and sweet smell of strong tea. Like his chewing gum that he kept in his pocket, like the Grecian formula he used to have me comb into his hair. Like beef stew and mashed potatoes with lots of butter and extra pepper. Joseph Leo McGuire is everywhere here. Finally, he is here with me.

Ireland wasn't on my list of places to visit because it was *our* place to visit, my grandpa and me. He was third- or fourth-generation Irish, or second, I'm not really sure. We made a lot of promises to each other when I was growing up, like best friends always do, and Ireland was one of them. I promised him we'd see Ireland together and he promised me he'd buy me a horse for my thirteenth birthday, so I guess we both turned out to be liars. Except he was everywhere here. Right away I feel him and my nana too, but mostly him. In the doilies on the side tables in the sitting room in my rented three-bedroom house. In the kitchen where there are canisters filled with instant coffee and tea bags and individual-sized Kit Kats and a sink that looks out over the back garden. He's with me when my host, Andy, picks me up at the airport because a woman shouldn't have to find her own way on her first night in a new city. When he drives me to the Tesco to get my now compulsory bottle of wine on arrival, smiling indulgently. Just like Joe McGuire always smiled at me.

My first morning, I wake up and eat a piece of white toast with butter and a soft-boiled egg with lots of salt and pepper. Two cups of tea but no coffee. If there was bacon I'd eat it too, but there isn't, so I dip my toast in my egg and set my tea cup on my doily. I wish I had a newspaper. I haven't read a newspaper in ages, since before I left Canada, which is sort of terrible I suppose. Nick got the *Saturday Star* every week so we could do the crosswords together and sometimes I'd check out the recipes or the "Dating Diaries" for fun but this wasn't a ritual for me. I wish it was a ritual for me. I wish Joe McGuire was here sitting across from me with the newspaper carefully folded at his elbow. We wouldn't talk at all to each other. Sometimes he might clear his throat or take a very loud slurp of his tea or blow his nose in his handkerchief, which was always, always disgusting to me. He'd be wearing pyjamas, like me, but his would be ironed and pilling from use. He'd wear slippers on his feet and a cardigan over his pyjamas buttoned over his belly. He'd cross one delicate, hairless ankle over his knee. His hair would be standing up on his head, his glasses on his nose. He is everywhere here.

It's a ridiculous thing for a woman in her forties to miss her grandfather, I suspect. Especially when he died almost twenty years ago, when my Jack was just a soft little baby at my breast still. But he was my first best friend, and I think I was his last best friend. When he died, we were in the middle of building a house together, a basement for him and an upstairs for me and my family. My husband was coming too, but really it was my grandpa and me and the kids. We found a place to buy good butter tarts close to the house. We took Cal and Ben to their new school together in the mornings. We drove around with baby Jack to look at furniture and appliances. Our lives were two sides of a shiny new penny until someone dropped it down the drain.

Joe McGuire died of a massive coronary. He died instantly. He just dropped to the ground and he died. He was seventy-three years old. He died before we could move into our new house together. He died before I left my husband, and this breaks my heart because he dearly wanted me to leave my husband. He died before he could meet Nathan. He died before he could see Ireland with his own eyes. At his funeral a woman sang "Danny Boy" a cappella as his body was taken out of a church, and everyone sobbed, and he would have loved that. Not the church, he would have loved the song and the sobbing. A month after he died, I found out I was pregnant with Nathan, and I named him Nathan Joseph. He would have loved that. He would have preferred Joseph Nathan and he would have preferred it if I gave him my last name of McGuire, but still, he would have loved it.

I miss my grandpa the way I think a person probably misses their dad. When kids in our neighbourhood talked about how tough their dads were, I always said, "I bet my grandpa could beat up your dad." And if he heard me, he'd say, "Whoa, hold on there." I didn't have a dad to include in the contest so he was my choice. I miss him like I miss my best friend. I forgot how much he was my best friend until Belfast. When I take a walk on the wet, warm sidewalks here, which give off a faint whiff of creosote, I can feel his hand on my back teaching me how to ride my bike. Up and down the street, both of us wearing shorts and baseball caps because I ached to be just like him. I even called myself Jimmy, tucking my braid under my hat, swearing I was a boy like him for many years. He'd read his newspaper on the porch until I said to him, "Why don't you go ahead and take me to the store for a treat?" and he'd sigh and fold up his sports section and take me wherever I wanted to go. He always took me where I wanted to go. To the store or to the mall or to the airport or just all over the back roads after a fight with my mom. With the windows down and we'd talk and talk and talk with the laziest voices you ever did hear.

I didn't want to come to Ireland all that much. Not at first. I suppose you could say I thought I came here to eat eggs and toast in Belfast for Joe McGuire. I thought I came here for him, for his namesake, Nathan, and for him. And sitting in the living room with my eggshells and crusts of white toast, with the grandfather clock ticking heavy in my ear, with the thick carpets and dark wood and taste of strong sweet tea on my tongue, I see. He took me where I wanted to go.

Laundromat Confessions

In Belfast there is a dryer for my personal use set in the room off the kitchen where there's also a stove and a fridge. The washer is in the kitchen under the sink. This is my first chance to dry clothes in a few months, so I wash and dry a load of socks and jeans that need to do that snugging up thing, so they fit my hips a bit better again. I dry them after I learn how to hook up a vent tube to push all that hot sock and underwear air to the outside, which isn't done automatically here. This dryer and my temporary use of it call laundromats to mind. It's the smell of it, the smell that isn't mine and yet it is sort of mine since it comes from drying my long-sleeved t-shirts and my pyjamas and my black cotton underwear with the waistbands pulling apart. There is a remembered smell of other people's clothes that have tumbled around in this dryer, things like tea towels and sheets since this house was owned by Andy's granny.

When we first moved to Owen Sound after I left David, we didn't have a dryer. Our house was the nice kind then, a townhouse with a little porch and a big eat-in kitchen. Two bathrooms and three bedrooms and two gas fireplaces. But there was just a washer that didn't work too well, always leaving the clothes one-third wet where I had to try to wring them out before I could hang them, but they never really felt dry. I'd look at Nathan's and Jack's little hand-knit sweaters, the kind that looked like they were made by loving grandmothers but were actually bought at Christmas craft sales, and think they'd never be right again. And there was something about the slow *drip-drip* of their sweaters into our bathtub, where they hung on the shower curtain, that would fill me with a particular kind of despair. I'd look at their small jeans, their individual tiny socks that never came quite clean on the soles, their Spider-Man underwear, and I'd wonder what would happen if all their clothes stayed wet like this forever.

This was around the time when I was in the thick of things with some horrible insomnia. Nights of watching Citytv until four in the morning, and trust me, there was nothing good on, ever. Most nights I'd end up begging myself to sleep for just a few hours. Just until the kids woke up at 7:00 a.m. and we all had to be our busy selves for sixteen hours or so. Sleep didn't come for me. For two months I might have slept about an hour or so a night, and I was so delirious that every morning I'd stare at the tops of the boys' heads as they ate their cereal and wonder where they could possibly have come from and when their parents might come pick them up and if I'd ever be finished babysitting. Sometimes I really wanted to be finished babysitting.

I gave up on the washer at that house after a month and decided to take our clothes to the laundromat. Sunrise Laundromat, three blocks from Cal and Ben's school. We had one laundry day per week, usually a Wednesday since it was my day off, and we'd take a taxi on those mornings. When I first left Dave, we had a minivan, but he took it back eventually so we became foot-bound travellers. The kids didn't mind. I had a double stroller for Jack and Nathan, just two and three at the time, which worked out for strolls to the park or the convenience store or Tim Hortons or even the mall in a pinch. Not to school though, it was too far and too early for walking. I made a deal with the local taxi company that was so generous I'll probably remember it until I die; five mornings per week for thirty dollars paid on Fridays by cheque or cash only. A call for 8:35 a.m. got us to school exactly on time. The driver, Clayton, someone's bald dad and grandpa, was kind to us and careful to drop the boys off one block away so they didn't have to climb out of the back of his van taxi in front of their new friends. It was always such a painful thing to watch, their big backpacks getting stuck as they muscled their way from the third-row seating to throw themselves chest-first out of the sliding door, and then Nathan, always buckled into his cushy second-row captain's chair with the built-in car seat as we made our daily trip, would scream, "Brothers! Hugs!" Those sweet boys would turn around to hug him. Every morning.

On Wednesday mornings, Cal and Ben would be dropped off and the rest of us would continue on to Sunrise Laundromat, a clean little laundromat with no owner or even employee that I ever saw. It was sandwiched between a fish-and-chips restaurant called Captain John's and an insurance broker in a strip mall where there was also a Vince's Kwik-Mart. We usually had two garbage bags of laundry at least, since we were down to the ends of our clothes, Nathan wearing his favourite t-shirt that read Little Body, Big Attitude, with track pants and mismatched socks. Jack in jeans with a non-stylish rip in the knee and his

Caillou t-shirt, always wearing his watch that couldn't tell time. He was only three so neither could he. Clayton would put the car in park and help me carry our laundry in, sometimes doing a little skit with Jack where he pretended Jack was carrying the bag because he was too weak to do it alone. This bit made Jack giggle so hard his face went red. He would also take us to Tim Hortons for a coffee and some Timbits too and not tell his dispatcher so they wouldn't charge me an extra two dollars, a kindness that made me feel clean and human. Like I had a dad who drove me places, and the kids had a grandpa who loved them.

Inside the laundromat there were always at least two or three women of retirement age, some of them I knew by sight and some I didn't. If this was our first time in the laundromat together, they'd usually make the same face when they saw us, which said, "Great, here goes my relaxing day at the laundromat." Sad to see me carrying two garbage bags full of laundry, getting out of a taxi wearing some legging and long shirt combination that was as unflattering as it was cheap. My hair pulled back in one of those lazy ponytails that's also a bun from being pulled through the elastic halfway. We'd pile in with our laundry and our soap and our rolls of change and take over four machines at least, but this shouldn't have been a problem since there were sixteen washing machines. I counted. Once I'd filled our machines and gotten them started, I'd take Jack and Nathan for a walk to the convenience store for the big treat, the only reason they were willing to behave for several hours in a steamy, loud, soulless milky-white building: candy. Maybe one pack of Pokémon cards if I'd made enough in tips the night before, even though they weren't old enough to really enjoy them. They knew Cal and Ben loved them and that was enough. The boys would spend about ten minutes crouched low in front of the Sour Cherry Blasters and Swedish Berries and Popeye Cigarettes and Red Hot Lips. Every candy decision was their last, there was no past and there was no future. I tried to get them to each pick something different and share but it rarely worked. Jack would get chocolate and Nathan would get something gummy and I'd get a Snickers and a Diet Coke. Sometimes I'd also get a magazine if the boys brought some of their toys with them. *People* or *In Style* if I really wanted to dream. Sometimes I really wanted to dream about a big house with a porch. Navy-and-white-striped duvet covers on bunk beds with drawers full of clean clothes. Curtains on the windows and homemade ice cream in the freezer. Sometimes this hurt too much. Sometimes I didn't want to dream at all.

Back at the laundromat our empty trash bags were folded neatly on top of our washing machines and we'd wait for the big switchover to the dryers. And this was when we'd make our friends. Nathan and Jack were addicted to TV, like me, so the three of us would share one chair in front of the small colour TV alongside the older women. They watched either *Maury* or a soap opera or *The Today Show* or *Regis and Kathie Lee*. We watched with them in silence, good silence. A silence where we all decided to be pals without saying we were pals. A little laugh at something Regis said, a *tsk-tsk* at a storyline on *Young and the Restless* we just weren't buying, usually something with Nikki and Victor. Jack and Nathan slowly eating through their candy then pulling some of their action figures out of their pockets to play at one of the folding tables. The women there, they changed then. Every time they changed. Shifted. Made room for the little boys they felt sure would ruin their day. One time a woman, round and aged and low to the ground, brought cookies for them in a little

Christmas tin decorated with white snowmen and red bells. Nathan ate them right out of the tin, leaning against her lap and watching TV with her. She never told me her name, but one time I saw her smooth her hand over his little shoulders, quiet-like. The boys were so good, I can't tell you how good they were. All day at a laundromat watching soap operas with a bunch of adults. Never complaining. They'd only fight over who got to push the cart of our wet clothes to the dryer and who got to load it. They both wanted to be the best helper.

At the end of the day, we'd have two garbage bags full of folded clean clothes that smelled sweet like the spring-breeze dryer sheets I splurged on at the No Frills. We'd take a taxi home too since it was hard to walk with all the laundry. Wednesdays were our days of being our own little family, standing on our own two feet, with clean pyjamas to wear to bed that night and clean socks for the morning too.

In Belfast, I think of them as I watch my socks tumble dry. Alone.

The North Remembers

You ask, why Belfast? And I'll tell you, *Game of Thrones*. Joe McGuire, sure, but also *Game of Thrones*. For the boys and I, this was our common denominator, our favourite topic and our way back to each other. Nathan especially. No matter how far gone he was from me as a teenager, if I said to him, "I'm going for a hike to think about that theory that Tyrion might be a Targaryen," you'd better believe he'd lace up his shoes and come with me. Sunday nights were sacred to Nathan, Jack and me. I usually made some sort of dinner, like Philly cheesesteaks or a big pot of chili. If Nick was visiting or it was that one year we lived with him, he didn't exist to any of us for that hour or the hour after when we broke down what had just happened. If Callum and Ben were home, they were a part of our *Game of Thrones* circle, and if they weren't home we'd text each other throughout to make sure we were on the same page with our theories. During the famous Red Wedding scene that shocked us all since we hadn't read the books, Callum was working in British Columbia and all he texted us was *I'm lying in bed trying to gather my thoughts*. I co-parented with *Game of Thrones* for the last few years. I was bound to this show. And so, I decided to be a real saint and spend the last month of my getaway in Ireland. For Nathan and for my grandpa. And for *Game of Thrones*.

After I found Nathan a cheap flight to join me for my final two weeks in Europe, we started to plan for real. Part of me felt like I'd given something up. I'd never had any real interest in going to Ireland. It felt so regular to me. Too much like home probably. My family is from Ireland but not too recently, and I don't even know what region we're from. When I asked as a kid, my grandpa said, "County Cork?" like it was a *Jeopardy* question. My nana told me our people were horse thieves and my mom told me that was probably a lie, but she didn't have the truth to replace the lie. I know our people are Duggans and O'Briens and McGuires and Matthews. I know we eat a lot of cake and make too many stews and love roasted potatoes. But other than that, I never had much interest in Ireland.

When I arrived in Belfast, I felt like I did something right for my son, this is true. After so many wrong turns and a few accidental right ones, it felt important to choose to do this for him. His cousin Jordan is flying over with him, which will help with his anxiety. I know Nathan is nervous about the flight but so excited about Ireland. I know he feels loved. I think that's it. I think that's the point. He feels loved by this choice I made for him. He feels like I'm choosing him. I see it in every message he sends me. Every text and phone call and every photo of his new haircut and question about school assignments.

But I feel I cheated, right or wrong, my time off cut short. For that new little seed of a me, that's just getting watered and given enough sunlight to sprout a bud or two, things seemed to have screeched to a halt. I'm staying just down the street from a Tesco where I can buy groceries that mostly look like groceries in Canada, except they are so very, very expensive. I'm back to paying speakeasy money for blueberries to put in my cereal. I notice this and the wine right away. After three months of drowning myself in crisp Italian whites and French rosés so clear and dry I've never tasted anything quite like them, I'm spoiled. I've gotten accustomed to paying for delicious wines that were cheaper than buying a two-litre bottle of pop at home. At the off-licence down the road, I bought white wine for about fifteen dollars and it wasn't good. That's all I'll say, I guess; it really just wasn't good.

I spoke to all the boys separately my first night in Belfast. By then their flights and our travel arrangements were booked and booked again after WOW Air collapsed and their flights were cancelled. It was a harrowing twenty-four hours when that happened, but I was in Avignon then and everything felt rosier. Nathan especially wanted to know what I thought of Belfast and I lied and said I thought it was great. The other boys asked too, and I didn't lie as much. But still I protected them from what I thought would be a deflating last month of a trip that was supposed to change my life.

That first night in Ireland, I wasn't ready to think Belfast was great. I was only ready to sulk and resent the end of choosing for myself. I didn't want to like Belfast.

I tell you this so you will know I'm almost always wrong about everything. Especially at first.

Cave Hill

My hiking guide, Andrea, pulls up in her Mini Cooper and parks in front of Belfast Castle with her dog, Honey. Andrea has more red curls than anyone but a Disney princess. I've paid her thirty pounds to take me up to the top of Cave Hill and tell me about Belfast history on my first entire day off from working in Ireland. Before meeting Andrea, I cooked a beef stew and felt very sorry for myself. No market, no bike rides, no sunshine, no Liza, no French that made me feel like a lighter, better version of myself. No Luca and no Angela and no Italian even, and I could still remember a little bit of Italian.

The Belfast neighbourhood I live in looks a lot like the neighbourhood where I grew up, actually, on 14th Street West with my grandparents and mom and little brothers and sometimes aunts or uncles. This house looks just like that house, doilies on end tables that are yellowed at the edges from old smoke. Tiny salt and pepper shakers made out of glass, juice cups in the cupboard that hold enough liquid for one small mouthful. An armchair of worn velvet sitting in the front window, looking out over a street of all the same houses. All brick, all flat-fronted, all the front lawns decorated mostly with recycling bins. Probably early spring flowers too, but all I decide to see are recycling bins. I am one of the first people to rent this house, Andy told me when he collected me from the airport. He and his brother hadn't changed anything in it. "It was our nan's you see. We didn't want to sell but we didn't know how to change it either, so we thought to give this lark a try."

I told him I loved it when he took me on a tour of the house, but it was a lie then. Even though he left me with fresh eggs and milk and tea and bread, I was sulky. Even though I had a choice of three bedrooms and excellent internet and the most comfortable bed yet, I couldn't let myself relax into the familiarity of this place. I didn't want a place to be familiar, I guess. I wanted to focus on a different version of me, not be reminded of the eight-year-old version of me playing hours of Chip Rummy with my nana at our dining room table. Eating slices of garlic bologna wrapped around a piece of old cheddar topped with mustard like we invented a new delicacy.

The house in Belfast holds ghosts in every corner. Some are mine and some aren't. I drink cups of tea in the armchair to the *tick-tick* of an old clock I can't see. The pink carpet, thick and clean and *hush-hushing* every one of my footsteps. My first days in Belfast were spent walking my new neighbourhood and listening to a British mystery audiobook. Every smile sent my way was sent back with a full stop, a smile that meant *No more smiles thank you.* I was so very busy refusing to accept that my new adventure was over, my new door closed. I decided to book a hike with Andrea because I could see Cave Hill looming over my neighbourhood from every angle and figured I should find a good place to go for walks straight away.

It was pouring when I woke this morning, enough rain that I thought we might not go for a hike, but when I contacted Andrea to see if she wanted to cancel, she responded, *Lol, you're in Ireland now might want to get used to the rain. See you at ten.*

So I'm wearing a raincoat and Blundstones and leggings and warm socks and a wool hat. Andrea is in full rain gear and she's brought me pants to try too. One of my fears is trying to fit into pants that are considered "universal size" and discovering that my size is somewhere out beyond the universe, so I say no thank you. Andrea is busy trying to get all her hair under a hat and shrugs, most of her curls still bulging out from beneath.

We hike through Cave Hill for about two hours. We climb past a small stream with water so clean, Andrea insists I bend down to drink some. I drink some alongside her dog, Honey, who laps it up with relish. We climb through mist to the famous caves, the ones that inspired *Gulliver's Travels*. The caves where Catholic priests once held secret, forbidden masses in the nooks and crannies, hoping the red coats roaming the hills wouldn't find them and put a stop to it. We climb and talk and become old friends in an hour. Just like that. Andrea is around my age and used to write for an Irish Republican newspaper. After that ended, she got into the business of having several jobs, like taking groups hiking, selling natural skin-care products for older ladies and working at a dog park. She's newly married to a man named Jonathan but she calls him Bones.

Andrea is a natural storyteller, the kind of person who sees all the ridiculous parts of herself and others but with so much affection. So much love. She's pissed off at all the same things that piss me off. She asks too many questions. The right sort of too many questions, where it feels like she just isn't editing herself. We are different and the same and delighted about it, openly delighted to meet each other. Me more than her, but still a little bit her.

We make it to the top of Cave Hill, McArt's Fort. Soaked through, I regret my refusal of those rain pants, my gloves too wet to wear. Our hats barely hold on as the wind whips around us, breathing out of our mouths in visible puffs. We're above the mist here, resting for a moment against old Druid rocks where the rebels of Belfast once plotted to take over the city from the red coats. This is where I first feel a low hum of something for Belfast. This is where a missing piece of me might have decided to wake up finally, sniffing the cold wet air. This is where I start to recognize an old part of myself that can breathe and breathe and breathe a little better here. I'm quiet for a minute, a first on our hike. She says, "I know, it's powerful stuff here, isn't it." When I just nod, she says, "It's okay, I understand how you feel. This place is in your blood."

She knows my heritage is Irish, but I'm Canadian from a long way back. Canadian my whole life and for generations before me. I'm not interested in trying to claim my Irish heritage like those people who wear *Kiss Me I'm Irish* t-shirts or those girls with the bright-green shamrock temporary tattoos on their cheeks ordering green beer on St. Patrick's Day. Before I went to Ireland, I met Irish people in Canada who all told me not to be that kind of tourist. Not to head over to the Emerald Isle and tell everyone you were Irish and expect them to throw you a party.

At the top of Cave Hill with Andrea, where the climb was hard and muddy and wet and the conversation flows without thought or reservation, I'm not sure what I feel. A drumming in the blood, a joy. A particular sort of joy I recognize and also don't.

Andrea drives me home from the walk, both of us soaked to the skin and talking about our tea and our stew and our showers at our homes that sound like the best things ever.

When she says, "So you're coming to my place on Saturday for dinner then, roast with Yorkshire puddings and the fixings," it never occurs to me to say no. Of course, I say yes. I offer to bring the wine and dessert, and we say goodbye, like, "See ya!" like it's no surprise at all that we've become friends so immediately. That we understand each other so well and so soon and so truly.

In my house, I warm up my stew on the stove as rain lashes at the windows. I have a long hot shower and switch into my sweats. I turn on the TV and watch *The Great British Baking Show* and decide to try out this version of myself.

Just to see.

He Had Yellow Eyes

At the Tesco that Thursday, I buy a bottle of pinot grigio, some Tayto sea-salt-and-malt-vinegar chips and a bag of mini Mars bars. If I were in a movie, the cashier would say, "You must be having a party!" But in a movie, I wouldn't be covered in mud. My pants are torn down the inseam, the kind of tear that's jagged from sliding down a muddy hill clutching at twigs and leaves. My track pants started out black but are now a sort of Australian shepherd mix of colours, brown and black and ecru where my leg flesh is visible. There's mud everywhere, on my elbows and in my hair and in the curve of both my ears. On the collar of my shirt and down my back, and I'm pretty certain inside my bra, where it itches terribly but I don't feel able to scratch my breast, not at the Tesco.

The cashier doesn't look surprised to see me so mud-covered. I have to assume that's only because she doesn't know me and is being polite. As far as she knows, I might be the sort of person who looks like this every day, covered in mud from head to foot like a toddler making mud pies in the backyard. She just smiles sort of blankly and says, "Do you need a bag, love?" I tell her I do and then I blurt out, "I just got lost for three hours in Cave Hill. I had no idea where I was and there was no one around anywhere. Three hours."

After hiking with Andrea the first time, I decided that winding my way up through Cave Hill would become my daily climb in Belfast. I made sure my phone was charged and had a fresh podcast and wore my most comfortable shoes and headed out for what I figured would be about an hour walk. Getting there was easy, Cave Hill is visible from everywhere in North Belfast, and everyone knows how to find it. I decided to climb the opposite way that Andrea and I had taken, to challenge myself. I made this decision knowing that my sense of direction is comically horrible. I've gotten lost in every city I've ever visited. I got lost after dropping Callum off at the University of Toronto his first year of school. His girlfriend, Amy, was in the car with me, and we were both so shell-shocked with loss, with the horror of leaving our golden boy behind to stare after us as we drove away in my minivan with the loud muffler, that we couldn't find our way home. I also got lost dropping Ben off at McMaster, Jack at York, Nathan at McMaster again and, oh boy, was that embarrassing since Ben had already been in Hamilton for several years. It was the shock of losing each boy to each school, but it was also me.

When I walked through the neighbourhoods of North Belfast that morning, I found my way just fine and I followed the path up the hill easily enough, up and up and up some more. It helped that there were plenty of people out on the trail enjoying the sunshine. I knew this because almost every person I passed, whether they were alone or in a group, called out, "Great day for a walk isn't it?" or "How much are you loving this sunshine?" My walk was a joyful sweaty one. When I got to the top of Cave Hill and stood at the old stones,

I decided to keep going instead of turning around and following the same path. Again, with the full knowledge that I have no sense of direction.

I walked until I noticed I hadn't seen anyone in about forty-five minutes. The last people I saw were two young girls sitting on their coats just under the caves. They were getting some sun on their shoulders with their heads down, and when I asked them if I was going in the right direction, they said words I knew were English but didn't understand. I was too uncomfortable to admit their accents were a mystery to me, so I continued on what looked like a path but wasn't a path for people. It was a path for cows or horses or some other four-legged animal but not two-legged women, like me. The path eventually tapered off into mud, and when I tried to follow it up again, I found myself sliding down the side of some sort of embankment, silently grasping at twigs and twisting my ankle so hard I thought I might not be able to walk. When I finally stopped, I sat against a damp stump covered in moss about halfway down what looked to be a deep valley of trees and shadow. I looked at my ripped pants and thought how quickly it all changed. How easily I could have continued sliding down that hill. It reminded me of driving on icy roads with bald all-season tires back home in Ontario once. When I drove down a hill to Nick's cabin and pressed on my brakes and nothing at all happened. I kept going, sliding downhill. Danger coming so gently, so slowly. Just like that.

My ankle was sore and my pants were ripped but still I thought, *Okay, there are dozens of people out hiking and Cave Hill is a public park.* I climbed back up the hill, fistfuls of mud digging so deep under my fingernails it hurt right to the quick, until I made it to a bit of a path and went in the opposite direction. *Okay,* I thought, *okay.* It wasn't okay though. I was lying to myself. I walked for another hour and the limbs of trees got closer and closer, the trunks thicker and thicker. I had to stare at my feet to make sure I didn't trip since my ankle was already sore and I didn't want to risk real injury. The sun was still strong, but I couldn't see it much, just hints of it through the forest ceiling. The podcast I'd been listening to was over, so I didn't have any voices to keep me company or distract me from all the rustling in the leaves all around me. From every corner I could hear the rustling and decided it was probably squirrels. Definitely just squirrels. I thought about calling for help when I hit my second hour of being lost. I thought about calling Nick, like usual, but he couldn't help me here. I thought about calling the police to say, what? I'm lost in Cave Hill somewhere. Can you search until you find me please? I might have called if my phone was getting any service or if I knew how to call 911 in Ireland.

I was alone in this. And it was starting to occur to me that I wasn't equipped to be this kind of alone.

For about five, no, ten minutes, I thought about what would happen if I never found my way back. If it grew even darker than the dark that was just coming from the branches overhead, and I was still here, still walking, still alone in a forest with no way of knowing how to get out, I'd be in trouble. I thought about who might know I was missing, and the answer was no one. After five days in Ireland, I'd met a few people at pubs like White's Tavern and the Sunflower where I listened to music and drank beer and got involved in chatter, or *craic*, like they called it, but they didn't know me. Not well. Andrea would expect me for our Saturday night dinner, sure, but that wasn't until the next day. I could be dead by then. For about five, no, ten minutes, I thought about being dead by dinner. Dying while out for a hike in a public park on a trip that was selfish. So selfish. Dying away from my boys when they all needed me to help them keep growing up a little. I started to walk faster then, panicked and frantic. I wasn't done raising the boys, they still needed me, and here I was in some fucking park in Ireland on some victory lap for a race I hadn't yet finished. I wasn't done being their mom.

I kept walking until I found a fence that was chain-link with signs that said Keep Out but there was no goddamn way I was going to keep out. I wasn't finished with my kids. I left on this trip before I was finished. I needed to finish. I felt along the fence and followed it for ten minutes before I realized something was watching me. When I stopped to check my phone for service, I felt someone's eyes on me. Giving me that awful prickly neck feeling.

I turned to find a small monkey with his little people's fingers wrapped around the fence, observing me. He had long white hair like a troll doll sticking out the top of his head and a black face. His small chest covered in more white hair, all of it so thick and straight it looked like he'd just come from a professional blow-out at the salon. His eyes wise and sad but curious. Head cocked while he watched me, and I swear to you, I swear, he was drumming his fingers on the fence a little like an impatient businessman sitting behind his desk. Like he expected more from me, like he didn't want to see me leave or stay or see me at all, I couldn't tell you for sure.

And this was when I started to cry because I was seeing monkeys in Belfast. Because I was lost and losing my mind. Because I was never going to find my way ever, ever. I knew there shouldn't be a monkey and I ran backwards from him as he watched. He might have even picked his nose while he watched. I ran and stumbled back into the dark forest and cried so hard my throat hurt from it. Nearly another hour went by. I stopped crying because crying alone is more boring than anything. Sniffing and wiping your face with a muddy hand. It was dirty and boring. I told myself the monkey wasn't real. He couldn't be real. I couldn't be that lost. I wasn't.

Eventually, I found the back of a church where the fence had an opening with beer bottles and chip bags and one potentially used condom in a surprisingly neat pile at the base of a post. I climbed over all this, hobbled and ran across the parking lot, and found a grandmother walking her grandchildren home from the bus stop who told me how to get to Antrim Road. She pulled her granddaughter closer, a little girl of about four or so who watched me with that same curiosity I'd seen in the monkey I probably didn't really see. The grandmother pointed the way back and said, "Oh dear, you have a long walk ahead of you. But you'll make it, you're all right now."

I don't tell the cashier at Tesco any of these details when I finally find my way here to buy my treasures, and I'm glad because she tells me, "Well, you're not lost now are you? Could have been worse, been raining. The sun is shining after all." And she's right. The sun is still shining. It takes me two weeks to tell anyone about that monkey, though I tell the story of getting lost time and again. To Uber drivers, to Andrea and Bones and their friends over our roast beef dinner. I join Andrea's hiking group and tell the other walkers about my adventure as we sit down for our tea and scones after a Saturday climb through the Mourne Mountains, and everyone laughs. "How does a person get lost in Cave Hill?" one man says as we ate our scones.

"To be fair, it is enormous. And if you don't know your way, it would be terribly confusing." This comes from a soft-spoken woman called Eillish.

I smile gratefully at her and a few others who give me sympathy with my tea. And when they start discussing whether the 999 emergency services would have come to look for me or whether it would have been search and rescue (which is a different number entirely), I finally say, "I think I saw a monkey." There is silence for a long ten seconds. Then shout after shout of delighted laughter. "For God's sake, you were in behind Belfast Zoo! You must have thought you'd lost your damn mind!" There is a zoo. And a real live monkey. Called a cotton-top tamarin, apparently. It wasn't all in my head. I was lost, but I hadn't lost my mind. Andrea tells me, "If you'd kept walking you would have seen a tiger. Can you even imagine?"

I can.

In Twos and Threes

By the time Nathan is due to arrive in Belfast, I'm a member of two walking groups. The Dynamos, led by Andrea, is my challenging group. We've already climbed the Divis Mountain with the rain whipping our faces and dogs running everywhere. We climb Slieve Gullion in the Mourne Mountains on Saturday. Andrea and I drive together with her dog, Honey, in the back and take the country roads. We arrive ten minutes late, and Andrea bounds out of the car and says to the disgruntled crew, "Well? What are you waiting for, get off your duffs and let's go." We climb in the sunshine with about twenty people and just as many dogs running through our feet. We climb to the top of a mountain, past old stone walls and sheep grazing and streams until we find a patch of dry grass and have a picnic. I bring a ham-and-cheddar sandwich on thick Veda bread, a kind of sweet sandwich bread the colour of toffee, with an apple and a bag of Tayto crisps, this time the cheese-and-onion flavour. Andrea brings a sandwich and shares it with another walker who forgot hers. One of the dogs keeps trying to eat everyone's sandwiches but no one cares; we lie out in the grass with our hands behind our heads and smile. Sunshine. So much sunshine in Ireland in April this year.

My other group walks through East Belfast on Wednesdays, and in this group, I learn about the Troubles. I knew a little about the Troubles before I went but I mostly knew that most people think Belfast is too gritty and too dangerous. Still a bit wild and dirty and full of difficult people who can't stop fighting each other, over what, exactly? Being Catholic or Protestant, something that wouldn't even come up in conversation in Canada as far as I know.

Andrea gives me the Coles notes version of the Troubles from her perspective as a journalist and a Catholic. She was raised in a Catholic household in North Belfast where some of the bloodiest fighting happened. Whether she's still Catholic is anyone's guess. She tells me how the British Protestants want Northern Ireland to become part of the United Kingdom, and Catholic Nationalists want to live in a united Ireland. When I went over to her house for dinner that first dinner party, carrying my apple crisp and two bottles of white wine, she told me she was in a mixed marriage. She meant her husband is a Protestant. "Played drums in the Orange band marching up and down the street and the whole deal, can you credit it?"

Andrea and Bones live in a Victorian row house they're in the middle of modernizing with second-hand finds, a big industrial-looking kitchen with hanging pots, and a stove that takes up one entire wall. They got married two years earlier and give the impression of being happily settled. We ate roast beef with Yorkshire pudding and roasted root vegetables and bread, with their friends Daniel from Germany and Dominga from Italy, crowded around their dining room table. We ate and told stories, and all of Andrea's stories are better than anything. Her stories of being kidnapped by loyalists when she worked at the newspaper, bomb sales after stores were destroyed and, my favourite, the murder of a rooster called Horatio kept me so engrossed my ice cream melted. I could sit there for hours listening and so I did.

Andrea's version of the Troubles is my first taste but it won't be my last. When I arrived, I was told by my new landlord, Andy, not to ask about the Troubles if I was out in public since the truce is still so raw, so painful. It's true that it's still raw and painful but it's also true that everyone I meet wants to delve deeply into their own personal role in the Troubles the first chance they get. An Uber driver taking me to a pub in central Belfast: "It's a good thing what they've done in the Cathedral Quarter with the yoga and the gay bar and the like. After so many years of nothing, we need to bring in you tourists. Did I tell you about my next-door neighbour, love? No? Well, the thing is, he lost his brother to a bomb, and his mother, she just never got over it, you know? She was a beautiful singer, she was, and after she lost her son with no money to give him a proper wake, the poor thing just never sang again. Do you want to go drive by and see the place? Won't take a minute, won't charge you or nothing."

Or sitting at the Morning Star Pub writing in my journal and drinking a pint of some sort of pale ale, a handsome man in his mid-thirties sits beside me: "What are you doing in this pub, love? It's not for tourists." "Why?" I asked. "Because this is a dangerous place. You see that man there? He was an enforcer for the loyalists. Killed a lot of men." He left moments later, and the ex-murderer turned to me and said, "What are you doing over there? Writing me a love letter?" His grey hair in a ponytail, a smirk on his face. After a few hours, I joined him and his friends at the bar and listened to their stories, their tales of near danger and loss and regret, so long as I promised to keep them out of my journal. "Only love letters, pet. No more horror stories for me." The Morning Star has become my spot for dinner based on the excellent burgers and bartenders and men standing at the bar who are always ready to tell me a story off the record.

There was another man at a different pub, during a lull in the traditional music called a *fiddle dee dee* by the locals; I guess they never saw Scarlett O'Hara say exactly that in *Gone with the Wind*. This man carried shopping bags and sat down across from me at my table with a weary sigh and said, "You see this scar on my head? I was shot during the Troubles. Shot by accident, but it doesn't feel like an accident to me, you see? You see the way these things work?"

No one holds on to secrets about the Troubles, at least not anyone I meet. Several museums, including the City Hall, are dedicated to the history of the fighting in Northern Ireland. A bus tour takes tourists around the big sites for the Troubles, like the Europa Hotel, which everyone proudly says is the most bombed hotel in all of Europe. Black cabs take you on tours of all the devastated neighbourhoods, and the people who live there wave happily as they water their flowers in the front garden. Unoffended. People talk about the Troubles openly, easily, their heartbreak on their sleeve.

Andy, who was born in the east end of Belfast, told me about the Wednesday walking group that wanders the neighbourhoods where *The Lion, the Witch and the Wardrobe* writer, C. S. Lewis, grew up. Now every Wednesday I meet up with Davey, our walk leader, and the rest of the group for a walk through some nice neighbourhoods that were rebuilt since the Troubles. Conversation focuses on the new and the improved and the parks and the effort to make everyone's life better. Davey is a robust, good-looking man who favours shorts and swims in the Atlantic Ocean once a week year-round. The group is a mix of older men and women just looking to stay active and social. As one member, Steve, explained to me, "There's a real problem with mental health here, so we're just trying to stay connected to each other." Steve told me about Men's Sheds, a government initiative where old, abandoned sheds are repurposed to offer men a safe space to get together to hang out and play pool and "talk about their feelings because there's no shame in that, you know?"

For four Wednesdays, I join the group for long walks ending with sandwiches or scones and tea. Sometimes a few of us go for a delicious breakfast called a mini fry: a fried egg and sausage and bacon, potato bread and soda bread, plus one small, broiled tomato. We walk through the actual Hollow on our walks, the one Van Morrison sang about in "Brown Eyed Girl," and when I mention I love Van Morrison, one member rolls his eyes and says, "Don't get too excited. Went to school with him, he's a right asshole." This is the general Belfast consensus on Van Morrison, talented but a right asshole.

Our walks take us through a forest carpeted with bluebells, the ground uneven with twigs and twisted roots. We walk looking at our feet and the backs of each other's windbreakers. We walk in groups of twos and threes. Sometimes I branch off to walk single file, listening to the rhythm of conversation that isn't for me but not hidden from me either. Grocery lists and gentle gossip and recipes for banoffee pie. We walk through an old cemetery, past an abandoned school and across a questionable rope bridge that makes everyone nervous, not just me.

I talk to a woman who just lost her son and is deciding whether to move to Edmonton to be closer to her daughter. Her son was disabled, taking up much of her time with his care, and she's lost without him. I can see how she's lost. I talk to another woman working on a book about her time as a psychiatric nurse, and she's too nervous to share too much. "I don't want to bore people," she tells me. "What if my story is boring?" Her story isn't boring so I tell her this in words I hope she believes. I tell her, "I don't know much about writing but I know I've met some really terrific women who write, and they always think they should shut up. I don't know if this is true for all women who are writers or women who are women, but I've found that people who worry about being boring usually aren't boring." She smiles away at something beyond my shoulder, maybe thinking about all her stories that aren't boring.

The closer the time comes for Nathan to arrive and my solitary adventure to end, the more I wonder about my walks. Not just the ones in groups, but my walks alone. Every day since that first day in Cave Hill, I walk the same path to the top. Every day, I think less about being alone and am simply alone. One day I join a *Game of Thrones* tour, an eight-hour jaunt that takes a busload of us to see some of the filming locations from the show, wander the Giant's Causeway, cross the Carrick-a-Rede rope bridge, and pass the Carrickfergus Castle. I pass the day in pleasant silence beside tourists who feel more like tourists than me. Mostly I walk along the rocky shores and through the little village of Cushendun, where I eat some good seafood chowder. And I guess I realize that I've learned more from walking in my whole wide life than I've learned from anything else.

As a little girl, I'd go for walks with my nana sometimes. There was a lilac bush in front of a house on my street and Nana and I used to walk there in our bare feet in the early evenings in June. Especially after it rained, and the branches were so thick with bunches of fragrant pale-purple flowers they were nearly touching the ground. We'd stand under it in the shade, the heady smell filling our lungs. My nana mostly wore a housedress, which looked so glamorous to me then. Like a woman on a postcard from Honolulu. She and I stood under the lilac bush that spilled out onto the sidewalk and breathed and breathed, her hand circling the air slowly to get more into our noses.

Sometimes in summer we walked the other way to the Pottawatomi River to get our feet wet, and we watched the minnows or sometimes a busy little salmon drift on by. Leaning back on our elbows with our faces tilted up to the sun, her short red curls not exactly right, but not exactly wrong either. I didn't know where my cousins were, or my brothers or my mom or my aunts or my uncles or my grandpa. I just knew that we could sit there and be quiet with each other, and that wasn't a thing that came naturally to either one of us. We dangled our feet and listened to the water and shut the hell up together until she'd lean forward, wipe the small stones from her hands and say, "How about we make some homemade eggnog?"

My nana had a talent for the ridiculous. Eggnog in August, tiny cucumber-and-cream-cheese sandwiches with the crusts cut off for dinner. Long conversations with my baby dolls about who they preferred as a great-grandparent, her or grandpa. The answer was always her because she did all the voices. When Prince Charles married Lady Diana Spencer, I was eleven years old and no one in our house seemed to care but us. We got up early in the morning to watch the wedding and eat biscuits with warm rhubarb preserves and drink tea and wonder which one of the princes I'd marry. "Edward," she decided. "Although I think

the little darling might be gay so we'll have to wait and see."
She loved talking about my future wedding, especially after
I promised her that she could be a bridesmaid. I felt sorry
for her when she told me she'd never been a bridesmaid
herself, married so young and everything, so I told her she
could be my bridesmaid and she never forgot. When I got
married to David, she asked me what colour my
bridesmaids would wear. I told her green, and she showed
up late to the ceremony wearing a lime-green dress with a
tropical silk sash belted around her middle. She walked
slowly down the aisle, just a few steps ahead of me. She
wasn't waiting for a second invitation.

I walked with my boys too, all the time. We walked to
school together in the mornings. I worked for an optometrist
for a while when Callum and Ben were in middle school, and
Jack and Nathan were in elementary. There wasn't a bus to
get them to school at the time because we'd moved to another
house on the other side of town. It was the first time a house
had enough bedrooms for everyone, and so we walked. They
said they hated it and maybe they did, I don't know. Some
days I hated it too, but not always. Sure, I remember trying to
get us all out the door in the mornings after eating our cereal
and making lunches, usually by about 8:15 a.m., everyone
flushed and rushed and hurried. I'd be knocking on Ben's and
Cal's doors like, "Time to get up, hon," and then, "Come on,
hon, your breakfast is ready!" and then, "Oh, for Christ's
sake, GET UP!" All of us mute with the long day ahead until
our feet hit the pavement outside our door and there was
nothing more to do but walk together. It was best in late
spring and early fall, when the air was crisp enough to need a
light coat. I wore scrubs and running shoes to the office, and
the boys, they were all old enough by this point. Their socks

matched, their clothes were clean enough, their permission slips signed, and even sometimes, they had some fresh baked cookies in their backpacks. The thing about me was that I baked. Flour, sugar and eggs were cheap, and so I baked, and so the boys knew I loved them.

On those walks in the morning, with everyone lined up wearing shoes without holes, and socks that matched, and homework finished in their backpacks, didn't we ever feel like a success. My body felt filled up with how full their bellies were and with the roast beef in the Crock-Pot that would be waiting for us that night. Our strides were long, Nathan's hand slipped in mine, inside his mitten or flesh on flesh. Jack dancing beside me with his stuck-up hair telling me a story with all those little additions of his, "and then," "and then." Callum telling me about a book he was reading and Ben telling me the songs he was practising on guitar with YouTube. They told me personal things too. The kind of sweet, tiny things they could only say when they didn't have to look me in the eye. They each found their turn, even if they had to fight for it, even if they had to yell over each other, so I could hear their truest thoughts. We walked in packs of twos and threes or sometimes one would walk single file if he needed his own time. If we walked fast enough on Friday mornings, we could make it to Tim Hortons for Timbits and I'd get two coffees to take to work, one for me and one for Keith, the optician. After dropping the kids off, I'd go to work and I'd be back at Jack and Nathan's school in time to walk them home. We'd stop at the Mill Dam to see if the salmon were running. Or we'd stop at the library and take out some books or stay at the school to play for so long my friend Laura would say, "Why don't we all just do dinner at my place tonight? Barbecue okay with you guys?" A lot of the time it was okay with us.

Here in Belfast, and I guess in Tivoli and Avignon, it's the same way with walking. I suppose I thought something grand might come from this trip. I packed two dresses in case something grand might happen, in case I was invited to a party at a villa outside Rome or maybe went out for a night of smoky jazz at a sexy club in Avignon. I wasn't sure what I was expecting other than I wanted to learn something about me and us and me again. I wanted to find a bud of a moment when everything became clear for me. When I'd learn how to stop being lonely, so desperately lonely, if my boys weren't in the room. Or learn how to stop loathing myself for all the things I didn't give them. The curtains on the windows of the home they were supposed to have forever instead of the mini blinds on windows of houses where they lived for six months or a year or two years at the most.

I almost forgave myself in my yoga class. I came very close one Thursday morning, at a studio in Belfast that offered first-timers unlimited classes for one month at a discounted rate. I love yoga but not in the way of people with excellent posture. No matter my weight, I've always loved the immediate gratification of yoga, of being able to stretch a little farther at the end of sixty minutes. Touching your toes instead of your ankles, clasping your elbows behind your back instead of your forearms. My yoga practice used to be about getting a yoga body. I could never enjoy the end part where we all nap together, it never made me happy. It never brought me anything except a laundry list of the other things I should be doing with my time instead of breathing and lying still. My class in Belfast, which I've visited about six times, is no better than any of the myriad classes I joined before. The sunrise yoga overlooking Georgian Bay. The classes I took in the basements of friends' houses where they charged me only five or ten dollars at a time and gave me a spiced tea at the end. All great, all worth it. I just wasn't there yet I guess.

But then something happened in my yoga class during our weekly meditation. Instead of thinking about breakfast after, where I walk to get my new favourite thing, the mini fry, and two cups of coffee, and I read the *Irish Times* at the table by the window, I stopped. I don't know why I stopped. We were sitting cross-legged instead of lying flat on our backs, this might be part of it. When we lie on our backs, I always think about my belly that's too round and my thighs that touch from knee to vagina. But we were sitting cross-legged with our eyes closed, and our teacher, Darryl, told us to put our hands on the pulse in our throat or over our hearts and concentrate on that pulse. He didn't ask me to use my third eye, which is great since that always makes me feel like a failure. I didn't have to try to breathe into my toenails. Instead, we just sat there breathing together, listening to our own hearts like it was the only thing. I listened to my heart with the palm of my hand, which I didn't know could happen but was happening. I listened to this heart that had always been my heart, even when I was a little girl swinging on the branches of a willow tree in the backyard.

I listened and I thought about the little girl I used to be, the little kid who just wanted everyone to be happy. The kid who walked to smell lilacs with her nana. I thought I wanted to forgive that little girl. I thought she tried her very best to make everyone just so happy.

I listened to my heartbeat. And for more than fifty beats I knew it was okay. I knew I'd tried my best.

14th Street West

Because my mother was a single mother and because she worked late nights as the bar manager at the Holiday Inn up on the hill, we lived with my grandparents when I was little. Most of my childhood we lived in the house on 14th Street West. I don't remember anything before living there except a few scenes, thirty-second commercials that weren't me but were also me. My first memory at a cottage at Sauble Beach, dark wood panelling and a ladder that led to a hot, windowless sleeping loft. I remember being lifted from a crib or a playpen or even a bed with the rails on the side by my mother. I think I was two years old only. She carried me to the steps outside this cottage on Lake Huron where I could hear the kind of laughter a person sometimes hears as a child that makes them want to go right back to sleep. Male laughter, bad laughter. My mother's hair was long and it smelled of something I'd later learn was Body On Tap, a shampoo made out of beer. She cried into my shoulder and kept saying, "I can't do this anymore, I can't do this anymore." I patted her back underneath her hair, still as a mouse except for that patting and soothing. And I said, "It's okay, Mommy."

Another commercial memory, the townhouse where we lived with my mother's first husband. The man she married when I was two, the father of my little brothers. She was in the galley kitchen making a tomato-soup cake, which tasted like carrot cake but without the carrots. It was afternoon, sunny and getting warm outside, like it was late spring. She wore some sort of loose, white top, and my stepdad came up behind her and pulled one of her breasts out of her top with his hand. The backs of his hands were covered with blonde hairs all over, and her face was so sad. She didn't stop him, she was just so sad. He locked me in a closet once too because I cried too much when she went to work, but all I remember from that day is darkness.

Otherwise, every memory starts at 14th Street West, the house of my grandparents. A brick house with two storeys and an attic that was my bedroom sometimes. The bedrooms always changed depending on who was living at home. My favourite was when the attic was my room on one side, and my mom and Aunt Brenda on the other, all of us divided by a wardrobe. The attic was warmed by a small electric heater that burned orange and smelled of singed cat hair, and the carpet was brown and worn thin by years of use, but I loved it up there. I had a small window on my side of the room that looked down at all the other houses on the street where I'd sit and read books or eat stolen fruit-on-the-bottom yogourts. The attic felt temporary in a way that pleased me, like we were always camping together inside a house even though I'd never been camping. My grandparents had separate bedrooms, even then, reportedly due to a snoring issue on both of their ends, which meant they took up two of the three bedrooms on the second floor. The third bedroom looked out over the willow tree in the backyard with two big, tall windows. So did the bathroom with the long sink and the mirrored shower doors, where I practised my moonwalk pretty successfully dozens of times.

There was no privacy on 14th Street West. If I was having a bath, my nana would often come in to pee and then my mom would wander in to start working on her makeup before heading to her job for the night. Then my Aunt Brenda would join to start her face, and my nana would stay, and it would be a party in there. I'd lie back in a tub full of bubbles that smelled of strawberry gum and listen in on the snippets of conversation they passed back and forth like a tube of good lipstick: "Did you see the Lambe's front porch lights? Almost exactly the same as ours. They really need to stop trying to compete with us, it's embarrassing for them." "Marge was at bridge on Monday and I just don't know what she's thinking. There's only so many crab salad sandwiches a person can eat." "Terry came into the bar last night with that new girlfriend of his, you should see her hair. Feathered bangs!" "Your father is at me about the chequebook again, why can't he just leave it alone already?"

Sometimes they talked about my real father, and sometimes if I was really quiet I'd get to hear clues that were never meant for me. He left before I was born, but it wasn't really any of my business, this was the part I knew for sure. But sometimes my mother would say, "I heard Bob Rouse bought a chain of Baskin-Robbins with his wife," and it would open up my world for a whole night. I'd picture a faceless man or maybe Tom Selleck or Robert Redford working away behind an ice cream counter. "Scoop of chocolate," he'd say to the local kids who dropped in with their moms after school. He'd be wearing one of those little hats people in old movies wore when they worked behind counters. The red-and-white striped kind. I pictured him being the kind of guy who smiled and acted silly and made all kids feel better because he listened to them all the way. I pictured kids saying, "Whoever has him as a dad is pretty lucky," and they wouldn't know it, but they would mean me.

I found out other things about my father when I was eavesdropping from the tub too. That he maybe had another child or two and he was raising at least one of them, a boy. That he was married, that he had brothers and a sister and a mom and a dad and some of those people lived a few blocks away. That he threatened to kill my mom if she didn't promise to have an abortion when she got pregnant with me. That he never wanted to see me and told my mom I'd probably be ugly because my family was so ugly. I liked the Baskin-Robbins story best.

The other best place in the house on 14th Street West was the kitchen. The women usually stayed in the kitchen or at the dining room table while the men, and there never seemed to be all that many, would stay in the living room. The kitchen had brown-and-orange linoleum on the floor, a window over the double sink and a telephone on the wall where everyone wrote down the phone numbers of their friends on the yellow-flowered wallpaper. My grandpa hated that a lot, especially when my aunts, who were in high school, scratched out their friends' names after a fight and then wrote them again when they made up. There was also a pop bottle opener on the wall that was so special, when someone painted the trim in an eggshell colour, they took their time painting the bottle opener too.

The men in our family didn't help with the cooking or the cleaning and they never said thank you for their food even though the women would take turns shouting, "Seriously?

Not even a thank you? Jesus." My grandfather spent most of his time in an armchair by the front window reading the newspaper or watching TV. A cup of cold tea at his elbow and either a cigarette or a cigar or a pipe or Nicorette gum in his mouth, depending on how far along he was in his five-year plan to quit smoking. He got to pick what was on TV, lots of westerns and cop dramas, but this wasn't enough to stop me from feeling sorry for him and his two sons. They might be able to watch back-to-back episodes of *The Rockford Files* while they waited for hot beef sandwiches served on TV trays, but they missed out on everything. On the small snacks my mom and my aunts and my nana made for themselves while they cooked, the burned end of the beef, salted and eaten on a piece of fresh bread and butter. Cottage cheese with cut-up canned peaches. Cup after cup of tea they served themselves first. A wedge of apple pie with a mound of vanilla ice cream while they played cards around the table and ignored the dishes for hours. "They're not going anywhere," was what they'd say. Sometimes if my grandfather asked for dessert, he was told, "Kitchen is closed," and they all laughed, except for him. The men in our family were people who drove cars and needed to be reminded to mow the lawn and were given the floor at the dinner table to tell a story for a maximum of five minutes. If they took more than five minutes, the women yelled over them. Usually about that one cousin no one seemed to like — and they all really liked not liking her. This was the way for the women in my family, they liked not liking things together.

They were so loud no matter what they were doing, laughing or crying or fighting. They fought too but not really. If one aunt was mad at another because she made some crack about how her kid did better in school, she never said a word to that aunt. That wasn't how it was done. She told her sister, who told my nana, who mentioned it to the perpetrator who said, "What the hell is she talking about? I never said that!" Then it all came back around to first aunt who said, "I know what I heard, she was basically saying my kid is stupid and it's always like this with everyone, acting like her kids are perfect and my kids are monsters." As a little kid, I heard about these fights and every time I figured that would be it, the end of our family. I thought the things they said behind each other's backs were the true things and whatever they said to each other in person was the lie, but this was wrong. It was all true, and all a lie. I couldn't follow the line of loyalty because there wasn't just one, each sister and mother and daughter combination was just as sly as the next. Was just as quick to take offence or give offence, quick to point out that one sister was still wearing size 14 jeans almost two years after giving birth, or another sister just broke up with another boyfriend and now what would she do? She wouldn't be young forever. I didn't understand then that they loved each other fiercely, more than anyone. They loved each other, I think, sometimes more than they loved us, their children. When my aunts came home for the weekends, my mom would go to bed early on a Thursday night in preparation to stay up late with them on a Friday, like it was Christmas. We were put to bed early so the adults could be all together without the children, and always they ordered pizza from Pizza Delight after I'd gone to bed. I could smell it from my room in the attic. They got Hawaiian pizza with green olives, so even if there were leftovers the kids would surely not be willing to eat any of it. On Saturday mornings before we were even out of bed, the moms and my nana were gone to the farmers market to buy sticky buns and rhubarb and steaks and new potatoes. My brothers and I got

our own cereal, and every time I checked to see if there was
even one slice of pizza left in the box, and every time there
were only shrivelled-up green olives and stringy pineapple
pieces covered in pizza sauce. I see now that my mom and her
sisters were so young then, all in their twenties. Made younger
still when they were together. They weren't ready to be moms
first and sisters second. The weekends of my childhood on
14th Street West were the weekends of their childhood too.

They just happened to be the ones who could afford to
buy the pizzas.

A Real Colleen

Every Friday night I visit a different pub by myself. Tonight is an Irish-Republican pub called Madden's, recommended by Andrea. "You'll have to ring a doorbell to get in, and there are bars on the windows but don't let that put you off, pet, it's great *craic*." Andrea isn't a drinker in the way my Dutch friend, Marcella, never smokes pot. "It's tacky, basically it's just for the tourists," is how Marcella explained it and how I think Andrea would explain it too. The pints, the rough housing, the men with their war stories, and their wives keeping their dinners warm in the oven at home. A puppet show for the tourists.

The men at Madden's, and there are only men, don't know they're putting on a puppet show for the tourists, which is too bad because they're so very good at it. Especially a man called Aiden from Galway who wears a corduroy blazer and is beautifully morose. Aiden joins me at my table straight away by telling me he knows I have a boyfriend hidden away somewhere but would I mind if he sits with me for a bit? We sit together talking about all the disappointments in Aiden's life, all the times he was nearly happy but couldn't quite find his way. The women he could have loved, the careers he almost had, the family who could never accept him. Aiden sings me his tragic love song through three pints and we're joined now and then by other men who might as well have been Aiden too, sometimes in football shirts and sometimes in button downs with very worn collars. They sing of all their various laments until three men come in and form a sort of band. A fiddler and guitar player and someone with a tidy little accordion, and they play the only songs I want to hear. Tonight, I'm making friends I'll never see again. Aiden, who writes me a long note in Gaelic in my journal while I'm in the toilet. A note I won't translate because it feels more special this way. The three men from the band. I buy them a round of Guinness and we share a cab but don't go home together. There's no suggestion that we'll go home together.

Never once do I enter a pub with a friend, and never once do I leave without one. White's Tavern on a rainy afternoon, the peat fire fragrant in the hearth. Old men standing at the bar and one comes up to me to talk about cryptic crosswords before stopping and saying, "Do you know? You remind me of my wife when we were young." And I don't know his wife, but this feels like such a compliment. There's no music. It's dark, the ceiling low, the tables long, the seats uncomfortable. But that fire is just so warm. The men are so curious and clear-eyed and kind to me for no good reason other than this is who they are. Asking after my family, my holiday, my history. "You're a real colleen," one says. A real colleen.

The Sunflower Tavern still has a cage at the entrance to protect people from stray bullets, and most of the guests inside are so young. Long beards mix with tight buns of thick hair on the men. The walls are covered with photos of the Troubles, for the tourists, I suppose. For me too, I suppose.

At the Sunflower, I meet John and he's young, maybe twenty-three or twenty-four. He's slight and well dressed and reminds me of Jim, a man I dated for several years when the boys were young.

Jim lived in Toronto and I visited him once a month for a few years. We met when I was in Toronto visiting a friend. He was at a karaoke bar having a rye and ginger and I was waiting for something to happen, and then he happened. We kissed that night and decided to stay in touch, it was as simple as that. I told him about my boys and explained I didn't want him to know them and he said no problem, simple as that. I took the bus down on weekends when I could, packed a few nice pairs of underwear in a bag and stayed at his apartment at Yonge and Eglington that felt like a spa it was so quiet. So luxurious. Perhaps so regular too, plain walls and a big-screen TV with an Xbox and several fighting games piled on the carpet. Nothing else about my life was regular then, and so his quiet banality felt so exotic. Jim was a man who offered me a little amnesia sometimes. He took me for breakfast on Sundays and live music on Saturday nights. We were the same age and liked the same movies, the same music and might have worked out if our lives hadn't been so different.

We eventually broke up because of this, our comically different lives. We laughingly broke up after he called me to tell me about a Russian puppet opera he'd just attended with some of his friends in the city, but I couldn't answer the phone. I was busy getting lice out of my sons' hair and eventually my hair too. The older boys were sent home from school utterly mortified, Nathan scratching his head so bad he bled through his baseball cap. The lice shampoo was around forty dollars, and I had to ask my friend's husband to pick it up on his way home from work while I washed the kids' clothes and bedding and stuffed animals. I lined them all up by the bathtub with Saran Wrap around their heads to hold in the bugs and the shampoo meant to kill the bugs, hosing them off one by one. Getting out the little silver nit comb that came with the shampoo (I couldn't afford), raking it against their red tender scalps, until Jack put his head in his hands and wept like he was at a funeral. Callum was quiet with deep shame, sitting in his pyjamas staring out the living room window at the trees, wondering how he'd gotten lice. Wondering who might know about his lice at school, since the volunteer mom who was checking his hair in the hallway called over another volunteer and said, "You see? This one is riddled with lice, now you can see what the bugs look like." The boys gave me lice too, my long hair exactly the perfect colour for nits to burrow down and hide as long as they liked.

I missed Jim's calls because I was sitting with my head flipped upside down and raking the same comb through my hair. Wishing I could afford to get all our hair cropped short, but the lice shampoo and gas money I gave as a thank you to my friend's husband had already bled me dry. This was it for Jim and me. We understood then that there'd be no Russian puppet operas for me, and since he was bald, no lice for him. I never saw him again.

Young John wears a hat because he's prematurely bald too. He sits beside me at the Sunflower and introduces himself by saying, "Love the pigtails, by the way, they're quite adorable," and then we just talk about everything. About the nature of being American that neither one of us understands even though we can't stop trying to understand it. Like the popular kids from school who have a certain indefinable something we all wanted even though we don't, not really. We talk about music because the fiddle dee dee at the Sunflower that night is a mix of southern Americana and Irish traditional. Lots of soulful, slow fiddle and banjo. No singing. Never singing.

John tells me he's gay after he pretends to be interested in a woman and I let a beat fall between his lie and my response. He says, "Okay, I see which way the wind will blow with you." After this, he tells me he has a crush on the bartender, a young Viking-looking guy with an easy smile and a pointed beard who wears linen pants and a loose buttoned shirt that shows off his strong chest. I tell John he has good taste, and he smiles around the top of his glass like a cat. We don't leave our stools for hours and drink through our dinner until it's time for me to finally find a taxi home. We say we'll call but we don't want to, not really. Our night is exactly perfect as it is.

The Parting Glass

Easter Sunday is my last day alone before I'll become a mom in person again and Andrea wants to make it special. "I'll be round for you in the morning for an Easter fry up, and then you'll be off to Helen's mother's for dinner around four."

"Who's Helen?"

"The one you met when I ran into you up Cave Hill last week. With the dogs."

She and Bones invited me for breakfast, which isn't actually surprising since I've taken to hanging out at their place after our group hikes. Eating dinner, watching TV in her sitting room with her young dog, Honey, on my lap and her old dog, Bosco, at my feet. Breakfast with them, sure, but Easter dinner at Helen's mother's house when she's just a vague shadowy brunette memory? That's too far. I tell Andrea, "That's so sweet of her but really, breakfast will be good enough. I'm planning on eating chocolate and watching movies on Sunday as it is." She says, "Well, Helen and Paul are collecting you and they already have your address, so you're going. You can't say no."

Easter was never a big deal for me growing up, not like Christmas. My nana or my mom usually made a ham, which was my third favourite of the roasted meats after chicken and turkey. I never believed in the Easter Bunny because the gifts he left tended to be service based. Socks and underwear. Maybe a bit of sidewalk chalk or bubbles. A short set for me that was clearly chosen by my mother, since it was more feminine than anything I'd want, baseball caps for my brothers. Sometimes a skipping rope. Mostly I liked the chocolate bunny, but my mom would only let us eat the ears and the feet before she put it in the freezer to save for later, which was also called never.

When my boys were growing up, Easter was just as confusing for me. We made breakfast a bigger deal than usual, maybe one of those layered egg-and-cheese dishes if old cheddar was on sale at No Frills. But the gifts were never right, never on the same level as their friends' gifts. One year I managed to buy them some scooters, the Walmart kind that didn't last very long, and Cal and Ben had to put them together without a screwdriver. Other years I bought Pokémon cards, Playmobil sets, Star Wars Lego, even buckets and pails. I wasn't sure what the gifts were for or how to decorate or what I was even celebrating.

I try explaining this to Andrea at breakfast on Easter Sunday. We sit barefoot in her kitchen with the garden door open and the sun shining on us. It's unseasonably warm in Belfast for April. Bones wears shorts as he stands in the doorway calling out insults to the next-door neighbour over a football match from the night before. I can't make out who liked which team, but the next-door neighbour's team won, this much I can tell from the triumphant sound of her voice. There's a lot of "your man" this and "your man" that until Andrea calls out, "You two are going to end up killing each other one of these days, and I'll tell you I wouldn't mind a bit," while sliding some sausages onto my plate. She tells me Easter isn't much of a big deal here either but, "You don't want to spend your last day as a free woman doing nothing, do you?" I suppose I don't.

Helen shows up as we're finishing breakfast with her two big dogs who immediately get down to the business of fighting with Honey and Bosco. Helen and her husband, Paul, who walks in with one more dog about an hour after she arrives, run a salon in North Belfast. Helen's a little younger than me and pretty and funny and confident and honest right away, like so many people I meet in Ireland. Helen tells me about her mom, Hilary, the woman meant to be feeding me more food in a few hours. Hilary was a single mother herself. "She raised the five of us after my dad left," she explains, "and she was so good at it. He left when I was in my teens, and my mom, she was a teacher, and she just figured it out." It seems Hilary is a force, a woman who doesn't look back and lament about her rough road and has no interest in her children lamenting either. She forbids lamenting. Helen tells me it's one of the reasons she wants her to meet me. I guess when I ran into Helen and Andrea out for a hike that day, I gave her my full history right there on the trail. The elevator speech of my life, like I was applying for a job at the corporation of Helen. I have no memory of this, and I blame it on Ireland and all the telling of stories that goes on there. In the lineup at the Tesco, on the trails in the foggy mountains, before and after yoga class, at the pub, oh my God, at the pub. On the bus, in an Uber, at every small museum and restaurant and café where I buy scones. Everyone tells stories that are too personal, too messy, too difficult or funny or mournful to forget. Same as mine, I guess.

Helen tells me that her mother still won't say a word against her ex-husband, which is fine except that Helen has embraced mental-health awareness, like a lot of the other people in Northern Ireland. Like the quiet, homeless man I met on one of the Wednesday walks who said he'd been discussing the danger of self-isolating with his court-appointed therapist and feared he might be in danger of losing important connections with potential friends. Like the taxi driver who smoked out the window after I said I didn't mind, and he asked me about *the yoga.* He'd been considering meditation as a way of healing from the trauma of the Troubles and wondered if some extra mindfulness might help him get better. "Give me a ring after class and tell me if anything happened, might go in for it myself if it seems worth it. Not wearing those pants though." Helen wants to share a little enlightenment with her mom, and while she doesn't come out and tell me to spill my guts about my life, I understand I'll be singing for my supper. I'm relieved, sitting here, drinking tea with Helen and Andrea and the dogs running through our legs with squeaky toys punctuating our sentences. Relieved to know I can provide something for dinner beyond my bottle of wine.

Helen and Paul collect me as promised and bring along Paul's eighteen-year-old son, who sits in the back seat with me and suffers my many questions. The same questions every adult asks, even though I'm trying not to be like every adult. How's school? How are your friends? Do you have an after-school job? Do you like it? He's polite and reedy with a sweet smile and a hint of something that speaks to a certain kind of confidence, one that comes from being on the road to becoming a handsome man.

Hilary lives in a house that I feel sure I recognize from the movie adaptation of *Sense and Sensibility*. It was called Barton Cottage, the house where the Dashwood women relocated after Lord Dashwood died and left them penniless because they were women. Of course, the Dashwood version of being penniless was different from most. It was a stone house with huge windows with light streaming across whitewash panelled walls and working fireplaces in every room. Hilary's house is just like this, with a big eat-in kitchen overlooking the garden, all the counters groaning under the weight of an obscene amount of food.

I'm wearing a black turtleneck and black pants when I meet Hilary, whose hair is curled and lips painted red. I know I look like a server at a roadhouse restaurant. She wears a white blouse and a statement necklace and rings, so many rings. Her fingers sparkle perfectly in time with her delicate chandelier and the crystal champagne glasses that hold actual champagne. There are uncles and aunts on hand, a sister of Helen and two nephews. One of the nephews is a little boy of four. He wants nothing more than to open every Kinder Egg in the massive bowl of chocolate on the dining room table until he finds one with a plastic motorcycle inside, like the one his friends at school found. He doesn't want to eat anything else. Not the roast turkey with stuffing, not the cedar-plank salmon in dill sauce, not the ham, not the scalloped potatoes, not the eggplant Parmesan, not the roasted asparagus, not the mini new potatoes with rosemary, not the beet-and-goat-cheese salad. Just the Kinder Egg with the motorcycle.

Normally when I'm in a room with that many new people I take very small portions, little bits of whatever might look the healthiest, which I pick at sporadically, even if I'm ravenous.

But here I eat two plates of every kind of food on offer. I eat that turkey and the salmon, which is perhaps the best salmon I've ever eaten, and I'm from Canada where the salmon is excellent. I mean to ask Hilary, through mouthfuls of bright-pink fish, if she used a bit of maple syrup when she marinated, but I get distracted. I eat dinner rolls slathered in sweet butter. Roast turkey in gravy alongside two kinds of potatoes. Mounds of asparagus topped with homemade hollandaise. Salad and more salad in an herb vinaigrette that offered a perfect, snappy bite to the soft goat cheese. I don't look at anyone else's plate to see if I'm eating more than them, and if they look at my plate, I have no idea. It's such a fine day that we eat outside in Hilary's garden under a canopy. The kids run through the grass, their plates of half-eaten food abandoned at the table. An aunt and uncle who joined are getting ready to go on a holiday cruise through the Mediterranean so the conversation twists and coils around travel. Around speaking other languages and foreign countries and new adventures. As the sun starts to get lower and lower, as everyone leans back in their chairs and drops their napkins onto their dinner plates as the white flag of surrender, voices get slower. Languid. Talk of future travel, like Helen and Paul's upcoming trip to Africa, turns to past tales. Of getting lost in Spain, meeting a lover in Holland, decadent meals everywhere. Hilary, finally done her duties as hostess, comes to sit beside me for a chat. We're both rosy from the wine and the sun and the food. She's kicked off her shoes as I have. She lays an arm on the back of my chair and says, "So, I hear your man left you with four little ones? I know a little something about that."

She tells me about working all day in the school and then tutoring at night to make ends meet. She tells me about her son who was a problem and her daughters who didn't seem like problems, but she figures they were just better at hiding. She tells me about her ex-husband who didn't pay support and we clink our glasses like the saddest kind of cheer. Hilary seems young to me, maybe in her sixties, but the bright end of being in your sixties. She opens up, more than her daughter might realize. Helen watches us covertly out of the corner of her eye, hoping for some sort of sign that her mother is finally opening up. Many hours later, when she and Paul drive me home, I tell her Hilary was lovely, that the dinner was the best I've had in all of Ireland, that I can't believe my luck in meeting such very fine people. I don't tell her what her mother told me about her life as a single mother.

Mothers and daughters tell their own stories to each other, I think. My mother tells me the stories she wants me to hear, and I hear what I want to hear, just like Helen and Hilary. To Helen, Hilary is the old guard. A woman who doesn't speak ill of her man, even long after he stopped being her man. For Hilary, it's about something else. She doesn't speak ill of her ex-husband because she wants to protect her children. Even when they're in their forties, this is all she wants. To be the version of herself her kids need.

I spend my last night alone in Belfast preparing to get my child at the airport in Dublin the next morning. I buy him food I think he'll like after months of only buying things I might like. I prepare his room. Then I tuck into my bed in the back bedroom, which overlooks the garden and the table where I sometimes drink my afternoon tea when working. I answer a text from Andrea and another from Liza wishing me a happy Easter, and the same from Muriel and Luca and even Lavyrne, who's remembered me all the way back in Florida.

And I prepare to turn myself back into his version of me.

Mom Interrupted

Nathan doesn't like to fly. I think it's okay if I tell you this. The last time he flew anywhere he was about eight years old and we were visiting my mom in California. He hated it. His ears hurt when the air pressure inside the cabin changed and even when they didn't hurt, he kept thinking about what it would be like when they started to hurt again. His brothers watched movies, ate snacks I packed in their carry-ons and made a big deal about the drinks the flight attendants offered them. "I'd just love a Pepsi with ice please, ma'am." But Nathan held tight to my hand after that first flight, after he knew what would be coming for him. He didn't relax for seven hours and, of course, this meant I didn't relax for seven hours either.

I've spoken to Nathan pretty often since I've been in Europe. It feels pretty often to me. He's my youngest, which means I've already learned from his brothers how to leave them alone sometimes. When Callum went away, not to university but before university, when he moved to British Columbia to work with his dad for the winter, I was quite terrible at finding balance. Bringing him to the airport and leaving him to fly on his own left me sobbing so hard one of the security officers asked me, "Do you think you're going to be okay?" The two-hour drive home alone was a dangerous one, every song on the radio reminded me of Callum. The songs I tried to sing to him as a baby, "Sweet Baby James" and "Danny's Song." I felt like I had water in my ears and couldn't quite stand up properly. I wanted to call him and then fly him home, especially when his dad wrote me an email that read, *Looks like it's my turn to have him. Time to stop being a mommy's boy.* This was deeply menacing to me. I learned to stop calling him so much. I learned to keep up through easy texting about shows we liked or music he thought I should listen to. He'd send me playlists called *good cowboy music* and ask me for recipes until it was my turn to ask him for recipes.

I learned that Ben needed me differently when he went away to university. That he wouldn't call me when he was hungry and had no money for food. That he'd disappear into himself and drift away from me. I learned that fun texts wouldn't get through his fog, and he needed a particular combination of space and fierce, present love. We wouldn't talk on the phone for a few weeks, but when I drove down to Hamilton to pick him up from McMaster and had to wake him up by banging on his dorm door at one in the afternoon because he drank too much the night before, Ben would lift me with his hugs. With the relief of being loved.

When Jack left, he felt too old and too young. Old in the way of his checklists for what he needed in his room, his car that was better than mine, his determination to make things work for himself. Young in the way that he teared up a bit when I left him at his residence at York University. He didn't think I could see, but I saw. In the movies, parents are met with eye rolls only when they show their love, but this wasn't the case with Jack ever. He's always been quiet and steady in his affection. Kissing me good night even after his brothers stopped. A little boy watching me cry during movies with a nervous half-smile to make sure my tears weren't real. Jack was good at responding to texts and good at giving me information and bad, yes quite bad, at telling me how he felt. He came home a lot at first. He needed to be in a place where he didn't always have to be so good at everything, and that place was me.

Nathan struggled without me. This I knew even though he told me nothing because he didn't want to be the one to ruin my plot. He'd call me to ask for help with his homework even though he didn't need it or send me pictures of his new haircut where he looked a little embarrassed to be taking a selfie and sending it to his mom. Once he texted me when he had been watching home videos he'd never seen. *You're pregnant with Callum and carrying a cake.* I'd never been pregnant in front of Nathan. This was new to him and also, I was young. *You look like a kid.* This is true because I was a kid. Not yet twenty-one. *You look so young,* he said again. I had him when I was twenty-eight. I was still young, but this young was a different sort of young to him. I'd always been Mom to him, always a grown person. In that video, I was almost the same age as him. Younger than Callum and Ben. Younger than ever.

When Nathan's plane lands in Dublin, I do the thing where you stand in front of the arrivals gate and smile at every person who comes through the door until your smile lands on the right person. It takes some time, but eventually there he is.

And of course, I have no smile for him when the time comes, it's only tears in my lane. Of course, I run at him, and of course, he laughs a sort of embarrassed laugh and hugs me, and I cry into his shoulder with so much relief and shock and happiness I think I might never stop. His poor cousin, Jordan, who flew over for a holiday with him, stands just behind, looking like she doesn't know where she should be, and I hug her too for good measure, but the truth is there isn't a single person at the airport except for Nathan. His hair is long, his beard is thick, thicker than most adult men can grow. He wears a grey hooded sweatshirt and khaki pants that I probably bought him for Christmas. His handsomeness hits me in the face all at once. Back in Canada, I got used to Nathan being good-looking. But here in Ireland, with his dark hair and his high cheekbones and wide smile and light-blue eyes, he's so beautiful to me and everyone else. It can't just be me who sees it.

We catch the bus back to Belfast after getting a coffee and a muffin. It's jam-packed with people, so we can't sit together. Nathan and Jordan fall asleep and I try not to watch him sleep. Or I try to make sure no one catches me watching him sleep. I think about how much Nathan hates public transportation, how crowded places make him so nervous that he gets fidgety and anxious. I think about how much change scares him sometimes. And I think about how far he's come to join me for a month on a big adventure, even though he's nervous and worried. Farther than he's ever been in his life. He came here for me and for him and for me. He trusts me to make things good for him, even as he sits sleeping and clutching his backpack to his chest. For two weeks, it'll just be us, and then we'll fly to Paris to meet the rest of us, the other boys. Our exclamation point at the end of this four-month-long sentence.

The rest of this, I guess, is over.

Meatball Subs on the Sofa

Nathan and Jordan settle in their separate bedrooms, sleeping long and deep and restless that first night from what they tell me. In the morning, I make breakfast for everyone, eggs, white toast and tea. Nothing special but I butter Nathan's toast like I did when he was little. Cut on the diagonal and fashioned on his plate. He takes it without a word, immersed in the tiny world on his phone, and I don't complain. I don't want to be one of those middle-aged people who complains about kids being on their phones. It hurts though. You could say that this hurts.

For four months I was so far gone that the boys would sometimes text me, *What country are you in now? Lol.* I've never really been anywhere without them, period. But now, after four months of newness and change and becoming a different kind of me, I'm surprised at how boring I still am to my son. I forgot this part — that I'm really very boring to my kids.

The first night Nathan arrived he wanted to tell me everything I missed and wanted to hear everything he missed. That boy on that night was all eye contact and curiosity. "How do you say *thank you* in Italian? Because I'm pretty sure it's *grazie*, is that right? That's actually kind of amazing that you can speak Italian." He wanted to see everything in Ireland, he told me. He'd been reading up on Belfast and had a list of things he wanted to do. Drinking in pubs didn't make the list, he told me, even though he was old enough to drink, but he wouldn't mind visiting some cool pubs just to see what they looked like. I told him about the few friends I'd made, the pubs I visited, the small life I was learning to live on my own. He wanted to hear all of it. Until he didn't.

I think it happened in the middle of the night. The shut-off valve I forgot exists in my sons. The way their eyes slide from mine and down and down, until I'm talking to the tops of their heads while they look at their phones. But it just really hurt that after four months of new information, I was interesting only for an hour or two at the most. When I talk to Nick that night he says, "Geez, doll, don't let him make you feel bad. You're his mother, for God's sake. A boy has got to love his mom." Loving me isn't the problem.

I give up trying to talk over breakfast and decide to take him for a hike instead. Jordan stays behind to catch up on her sleep, so it's just us two and we find our groove as we walk. I take him down some of my favourite side streets to get over to Cave Hill. Terraced homes sit behind dry stone walls, and a private school looks the way we both pictured Yale might look even though we've never seen it. We talk about Rome and Tivoli. We talk about Avignon and my hikes in the mountains and new friends. When I say we talk, I mean I talk. And as we climb Cave Hill, I know I'm trying to sell Nathan on this new me. This me who isn't as afraid these days, and his eyes slide away because he's come here to be with the old me. The mom who listened to his problems, who picked him up from his after-school job at the Cineplex and shared a leftover movie-theatre hot dog with him. The one who asked him questions, who wanted to be his cheerleader. He wants me to be his cheerleader. He hasn't brought the proper attire to suddenly become *my* cheerleader and he doesn't have the right training. It's too much for him, after four months of no Mom to meet a new mom. Just too much.

And so I say, "Let's grab Subway for lunch." We get meatball subs after our hike and splurge on the cookies because they really do make the greatest cookies. We bring food home for Jordan too, and it starts to rain once we get back. The kind of rain that's so heavy it gives you permission to stay inside if that's the way you want to do it. Andy and Alan, the brothers renting me the house, have sent over one of those illegal boxes where you can watch anything you want. So, we watch Sunday night's episode of *Game of Thrones* together since we both missed it. We eat our subs on the sofa in the front room and save our cookies for later. We argue over what we think the ending of the series will be since it's the last season and so much of our lives have been leading up to this moment. Nathan thinks Daenerys is turning into an evil queen and he hopes she will since that's her character arc. "You can't just decide to change her character partway through the show, you know?"

I know.

King of the North

Nathan's a little mad at his hamburger. We're eating at the Morning Star at Pottinger's Entry, and I have a pint of some kind of pale ale the bartender recommended. I know the bartender like I know a few of the other men standing around the bar, but no one offers me more than a quick nod of the head when they see us. I'm a mom again. We both got the Morning Star burger topped with brandy and peppercorn sauce, not to mention the smoked cheese and french-fried onions served with a mound of homemade french fries that are all the same size and consistency. Lightly salted, no duds. Nathan eats his burger with his eyes half closed and doesn't talk, that's how good it is. But the price of it is making it taste around 30 percent worse for him. It's about eighteen dollars for the meal, which is obviously not a horrendously expensive price to pay, unless you're expected to pay for it yourself, even though your mom is sitting right there at the table with you.

Before I booked flights for the kids to come to Europe and before I spent six or seven hours on Hostelworld finding us two rooms for two nights in Montmartre in Paris and before I found an apartment for nearly two weeks in Rome on

Airbnb, I told them all one thing, "Your spending money is on you." And I meant it even though it made me blush with how bitchy it sounded. Even though I shouldn't have had to say it. But it's always been this way. Before we'd enter a restaurant, sometimes Montana's or East Side Mario's or the Harrison Park Inn after a game of mini-golf at the park, I'd tell the boys, "I have exactly fifteen dollars per person to spend here plus tip, so you do your own math when you're ordering." When they were little, they could order kids meals that came with drinks and desserts, and when I worked at Joe Tomato's we got a staff discount. Some days when I worked, I wouldn't eat my staff meal and my boss would say, "Bring the kids in for dinner, and we'll give you the same fifty percent off since you didn't get a chance to eat." When family came to town to visit, my mom or my aunts and uncles, they took turns taking us out for dinner. "Eat whatever you want" was the theme of these dinners, but my kids were still nervous to order too much. Still glanced at me anxiously around their menus and said things like, "I'm not that hungry," or "Ben and I were just going to share a pizza, is that okay?" They were different with their grandma, who came for weeks at a time from California and was just as excited about Harvey's hamburgers with extra onions and pickles as they were. They understood she wanted to treat them, and yes, sure, I'd love to treat them too, but it isn't always in the cards for me.

My budget is tight always, but for these four months especially. I still have a few bills I'm paying every month, a reduced rent, car loan, phone bill. I'm careful with my money. I buy very little and buy day passes for public transportation or walk or cycle when I can. I use the kitchens in my rentals and usually visit other towns on day trips instead of staying overnight. I knew I'd need to keep a little money aside to help the boys out when they got here but I also need to save money to fix my horrendously broken car when I get home.

That's waiting for me when I get home. I can't forget.

I want to pay for Nathan's burger but I don't. Not because I can't afford that one meal for him but because I'm afraid of the slide that will take place. When he was a little boy and wanted to carry two action figures plus a coat and sweatshirt and two snacks on a sunny walk through the zoo, I'd say, "Nathan, I'm not carrying any of this for you," and he'd agree. By the end of the day, my arms would be full of sweaters and action figures and granola bar packets I had no memory of accepting. It would be the same here, only with four boys instead of one. It would be, "Mom, can you grab my muffin?" and then, "Mom, I'm out of change. Can you just get my train ticket?" and then, "I probably won't eat because I can't afford it," which sinks me every time. This can't start, not already. If it does we'll all be sunk. And so, I just let Nathan's burger taste 30 percent less delicious.

Nathan isn't cheap. He just has his priorities for Ireland, and those priorities are *Game of Thrones* tours. Nathan and Jordan have planned to take the same tour together while I work, and then we decide on impulse, after one especially good episode, to splurge, to take the Winterfell tour. It's a day tour led by seasoned *Game of Thrones* extra Andy McClay, who's more passionate about the show than anything else in his life. He has a long beard and a grizzled face that Nathan and I both are certain we recognize from the show. When he meets us in the morning outside the Europa bus centre, he tells us straight away, "This tour is only for *Game of Thrones* fans. If you want to know the history of Inch Abbey or some shit like that, you're on the wrong fucking tour. I love this shit more than anything, and that's all we'll be talking about today, all right?" Andy goes on to tell us that he moved to Belfast from Londonderry when they started filming *Game of Thrones* and found an apartment close enough to Titanic Studios that he could be available for anything at a moment's notice. He also tells a story about an ex-girlfriend who didn't really like *Game of Thrones*. She liked *Gilmore Girls* instead, and so they broke up. Everyone on the bus laughs, but I can tell this is a true story. The whole city of Belfast seems to have a *Game of Thrones* story. Two women in their late sixties in my Wednesday walking group have been extras even though they don't watch the show. They just wanted to be a part of something that was special to Belfast. Every Uber driver I meet has driven some cast member or another, although half the time they don't know who they play, and it becomes a quick game of *Jeopardy* in the car with me saying, "Was he slightly chubby? Did she have very pronounced eyebrows and a winning smile? Was his hair in a ponytail?"

Our tour with Andy opens something up in Nathan. It validates his passion for *Game of Thrones* and his passion for the things he cares about in every part of his life, but it's more than that. Andy takes us through Tollymore Forest, a mystical, beautiful place where they've shot some scenes from the series. We go to Inch Abbey, and true to his word, Andy has no information about the tenth-century ruin. Instead, he pulls a box of cloaks and heavy, realistic swords out of the back of the bus and tells us to follow him to the abbey, where Robb Stark was once declared King of the North, to recreate the same scene. Nathan dives right in. I decline the costume, but Nathan wraps a faux fur-lined cloak around his shoulders and asks a fellow fan to trade swords with him because the broad sword he's carrying feels too awkward. He stands and screams,

"King of the North!" with the rest of the gang. I stand back and watch. I take video footage for him to share with his friends later. I'm his cheerleader. His supporting cast. His stenographer.

On the ride home on the bus, Nathan stares out the window seeing everything. He's quiet with more than *Game of Thrones*. He's watching the forests and the trees and the rivers, and he's feeling that thrum of something I feel too. That mystical something of Ireland. I relax back in my seat. He gets it.

Black Velvet Band

I spend my last few days in Belfast watching Nathan. I say goodbye to Andrea over breakfast one morning, but I'm distracted, gone already. She sees it too. I'm back in the bleachers. I'm an extra in the story. I don't say goodbye to Ireland at all. And worse, I never say thank you. I never take a minute to stand in all that Ireland has given me. In Ireland I found my people. In Ireland I found my stride. In Ireland I found my friend. My best friend, Joe McGuire. He was dead, long dead, but in Belfast he came back to me, and we were pals again. He and I were back together, not in the sad grown-up way but in the way when I was a girl. When we'd go for drives in the summer on the back roads up to Inglis Falls, and he'd let me sit on his lap and steer the car. He was in the kitchen getting some good steaks ready for the barbecue and asked me to come stand with him while he flipped. He was at the pub singing with his eyes closed, "Black Velvet Band" and "Belle of Belfast City" in his deep baritone. I lost my friend called grandpa for a long time, but he came back as easy as anything in Ireland.

I don't say goodbye to him, and I don't say goodbye to Ireland. I guess that's because I just can't. And I guess I know I'll come back.

Paris

My three other boys and Ben's girlfriend all arrived yesterday from Canada. Nathan and I collected them from the airport, and he told me I should definitely cry when I saw his brothers so they would know I missed them. Like I had any choice. Callum and Jack flew together on one flight, Ben and Jessica on another. They looked different: Callum looked older, Jack looked younger, Ben looked thinner. I clocked each slight change and worried about them for different reasons. But they arrived safely with their slightly stained, poorly packed carry-on bags and smiled with relief when they saw me, each of them. They hugged me, each of them. They came to Paris, each of them.

Paris is no one's choice but mine, and maybe Jessica's, but they play along since that's the theme of the past four months of our lives. I make decisions and they play along. I think this has been the theme of all our lives together until this moment. The hostel I found in Montmartre is good, young, bright and colourful, even in the rain that won't let up on our first day. We take an Uber from the airport to Montmartre that costs a fortune because we need what is essentially a minivan limousine. The rain makes Paris look dingy and the Russian driver is unhappy with us or the rain or the traffic. I can't be sure. All I know is that Paris looks about as appealing as one of those Jason Bourne movies except without the cool scenes of Matt Damon fighting. I try my French on the driver and also my charm, but he wants silence and frowning only. I look in the back seat to make eye contact with Cal, and he gives me the "give it a rest please" face, like he's the dad and I'm the kid. Callum, Jack, Nathan and I share a room with two sets of bunk beds and a private washroom, while Ben and Jessica have their own room. They told me I didn't have to book them a separate room, but I did it anyways to avoid conversations about sex.

Our hostel is close to the Sacré-Cœur Basilica, just down several flights of stairs that Nathan and I find as the rest of them sleep off their jet lag for a few hours. The church has a beautiful view of the city but it's crowded. This is Paris in the springtime just like Maurice Chevalier sang. We wander up and down side streets to find a good spot for dinner that might serve some vegan food for Ben and Jessica, but instead find warm croissants and *pains au chocolat* as a treat for the sleepers. We stop at a brasserie next to our hostel to eat sandwiches while we wait for them to wake up. Each of us dining on sandwiches like *croque-monsieurs* with Gruyère cheese and béchamel sauce plus a little bowl of french fries for sharing and a green salad too. I'm glad for him to see the kind of place where locals eat, with the big square-tiled floor and an old brass bar taking up nearly the entire restaurant. I'm glad to speak French in front of him too, though I don't exactly know why. His face gives me nothing.

Everyone wakes up before dinner and we watch the sun set from Ben and Jessica's room. It's nicer than ours, with a tiny Juliet balcony looking out over a busy Parisian street, like the kind you always wanted to see. Jack and Ben and Nathan and Jessica are sitting on the bed talking about their flights and their sleep and their plans for the next two weeks. Callum and I stand at the open window, not saying a word. Maybe he didn't want to come to Europe or it's possible he did want to come — but this isn't exactly the way I wanted it. We got into one of those weird messaging fights a few weeks before. It's the worst kind of fight to have, I think. When you watch the speech bubbles come up and pause and end, and you're red-faced with all the angry things you want to say but you don't know how to say them. We fought because I thought he was trying to back out of coming, and I couldn't bear it. I couldn't bear his absence on this trip that all started with him.

I don't know if it was because he was worried about money, worried about his job, worried about his girlfriend. Worried about all the parts of his life that didn't occur to me when I thought of this trip for all of us. The trip I first thought of when he and I were the only two parts of us. The trip I thought about when he was a baby boy with his chubby fists and sore red cheeks from teething. When he was asleep at my breast in the dingy apartment that I shared with his father. When we were nestled together in our one good chair enjoying the sunshine of an early spring afternoon alone, it always was the two of us alone. Even if there were people in the room, it was just him and me in those days. I looked at his face then and thought I wanted to show him the world. I didn't look at my apartment, where there were empty McDonald's containers peeking out of bags on the floor, where the carpet was dirty. Where I was living with a man I possibly didn't love and working part-time as a bartender in the local strip club and could barely afford our rent. I looked at his face then and thought he was the purest perfect thing. I decided that, for sure, I'd give him more. Not now and probably not for a long time, but some day. I was learning to be a grown-up then, but I knew I wanted more for him. I knew I'd need to say sorry for so much. I just knew it even then.

So, when I thought he was telling me he didn't want to come or couldn't come or needed not to come, I couldn't bear it. And I told him. And we fought, though I don't know what we said at all. I just know he said he'd come in the end. Maybe he was always going to come in the end, and maybe I invented this fear, it's still hard to tell. But he came. And that is everything.

We stand beside each other in the window in Paris, a forty-six-year-old mom and her twenty-five-year-old son. The happy buzz of his brothers and my sons in our ears. I pour a glass of wine for myself and some for him too. The sun is going down. It's a Friday evening. The light is the pink you always hope it's going to be in Paris. The rain has stopped. We stand quiet. Callum so much taller than me. His profile thoughtful. His face the same to me. Endlessly the same. And he says, "You know, Mom, I was always going to come. We've been talking about this since I was a little boy. You know it's always been you and me." And there he is.

We're walking along the river Seine looking for somewhere to pee. For me and possibly Jessica, though she hasn't said a word, I can just tell by the way she's walking. Jack's in charge of navigation with his phone and his tech skills but it isn't like he can just type *Where can my mom pee in Paris?* and get a listing. I know because I've asked. We are on the left bank and on our way to Boulevard Saint-Germain where I want to visit the same cafés where Hemingway and Picasso once sat. But first I have to pee really badly. I can't concentrate for thinking about peeing. I can't see the Seine or the Eiffel Tower without having peeing on the brain and it's ruining the experience. Nathan doesn't pee in public ever. He reminds me of this as we keep walking to look for a public washroom but all we see are stores, like Louis Vuitton and a Kiehl's that looks promising but isn't. "This is when it comes in handy," Nathan says. "I barely remember what it feels like to have to pee right now."

We walk all the way from Montmartre to the left bank to see Les Deux Magots, where Hemingway once wrote, and the only thing I can tell you is that you have to buy lunch if you want to pee in their washroom. I can't afford lunch. If it was just me at Les Deux Magots, I would stop to eat, maybe an endive tart and a mixed green salad with walnut vinaigrette and a glass of Beaujolais for €25. I'd use the washroom once and then again after I finish my *café crème* while sitting on the covered terrace facing out to the street. I'd wait for a seat on the terrace. It would be an expensive lunch for sure, more than I normally might like to spend. But sort of like Caffè Greco in Rome, this was one of those touristy experiences that might be worth it. I can't afford lunch for all of us at this restaurant or any of the others here. Lunch for six would come to well over €100, even if we stick to sandwiches and coffee or water. And as I discover almost immediately, no one seems to have much money. Not the kind of money where a person can just stop to eat wherever they like without thinking about it first. Without thinking of giving up on something else first.

Instead of buying lunch on our day of walking around Paris, we planned ahead. After breakfast, we found a little market and bought baguettes with a few wedges of strong cheese to eat as we walked around. Ben brought a Swiss Army knife for slicing the cheese, Jessica and Callum threw in some fresh strawberries and grapes as plump and round as plums, and Jack offered to carry all our food in the family backpack, along with his good camera, a bottle of wine and a bottle of water. This has allowed us to wander the whole day without worrying about finding a place to eat. We found a park with a carousel, a garden, a fountain and a little ice cream kiosk hidden behind old gates. There were marble statues and a small stage, and I thought we could have stayed there forever. The day was new, and we'd all slept so very well in our hostel and the sun came out to shine low and flattering on us, the good light of Paris finally. I bought us all an ice cream cone or a coffee but not both, I couldn't do both.

Our walk takes us past the Arc de Triomphe, the Musée d'Orsay, the Eiffel Tower of course. We don't go inside any of these places because they cost money, but still there are moments. When we walk in our Rubik's Cube combinations, two at a time, but this one with that one and that one with this one. When I have five or ten or fifteen minutes alone with each boy and one girl, that brave girl who didn't tiptoe into our family but leapt in with two feet. I worried about Jessica when she was the only girlfriend who could make the trip. She and Ben have been dating for about a year or so, and we all like her, thank God. I like all the girlfriends, thank God. I used to worry that my sons would find people who didn't want me to be one of their people. That they'd be men who shrugged, men who gave me up in layers until I was gone altogether. So far, this hasn't happened, but I know. I know it could. I've always known it could. I worried about Jess because we're so much to take on as a family. Even for Nick. When we're all with him, he takes many ten-minute naps that turn into thirty-minute ones. "It wouldn't be so bad if you were all talking about the same thing," he says. "But you're all so quick. You keep changing the subject before I have a chance to catch up." Jessica has spent the night with us a few times as a group and been to the cottage we rent at Sauble Beach, but two weeks in Europe could have been too much. Not yet. She holds her own. And as we walk around Paris, she talks to everyone. I catch a sight of her and Nathan with their heads bowed in conversation. She talks to Callum and he throws his head back to give one of his hard-won shouts of real laughter. She offers to take the backpack for Jack but he says no thank you, and they fall in step together. She is the sixth side of our Rubik's Cube here.

By the time we reach the Seine, we've been walking for two hours. We decide to rest and eat our lunch and drink our wine on a bench. We watch the tour boats drift up the river until I ruin it all and need to pee. It's odd how peeing shifts the dynamic in our group. How the boys are frustrated with me and say things like, "Why didn't you go before you left the hostel?" and "Are you sure you can't just hold it?" They don't understand because they have young people bladders, but no I can't hold it and I don't want to hold it. When I finally find a restaurant where I can get a coffee in exchange for peeing, they all follow me inside and order water so they can sit down. But the waiter at this restaurant, where the walls are deep red and the brass is legitimately shiny, tells them they have to order something to eat or drink, and by the time I come back from peeing, he tells me we can just leave, he understands. He tells me he knows the prices are steep. He knows it's difficult for women to pee in Paris, but men can just do it wherever. Walking out, I feel light as a feather.

We decide to cross back over the Seine. The rain starts again but this rain is just so different from the rain that makes everything look dingy. This rain is soft, the kind of rain that doesn't seem to get your clothes wet but makes everything misty, including a person's hair. The kids walk ahead of me on the Pont du Carrousel, where love locks line the bridge in great clusters of promises. As we get closer to the Louvre we hear violins, and under the entrance there are two men, one playing the violin and another singing opera. The smell of roasting chestnuts is here too. It's in the thin curls of smoke that seem to come up from the ground somewhere around our knees. We don't go inside the Louvre. "We can't afford it" — the same refrain but also something else. We're standing outside in the rain with the chestnut smoke and the opera-singing teenager, the violinist and the people in trench coats all around us with their heads tilted to the music. We can just see the obelisk to our right. We know where we are and how long it took us to get here. We stand in a moment that won't be better moving forward. Each of us is still, so still. I don't even take a picture of anyone, that's how much I want to remember.

No Blank Slate

After our weekend in Paris, we head to Rome. Our apartment in Rome isn't in Rome and it isn't in a cute village just outside Rome. It's on the bus line with a pizzeria and a grocery store and a café. I needed an apartment that would be close to town with lots of bedrooms and a kitchen. A person might think this would be easy but it wasn't. Not if you have only about $1500 to spend for two weeks, which is what I have. Back in Tivoli, I showed the apartment listing to Luca and Angela, and she frowned at my phone to say, "This one is not so good. It is at least forty-five minutes to get into the city centre. Jennifer, this is too far, you know this." When I told her this was all I could afford, she stopped herself from saying more. Angela is a lawyer. I don't know if lawyers make a lot of money in Italy like they do at home, but from the look on her face … probably.

The apartment is one of four in a complex owned by a whole family who spends the next two weeks spying on us in all sorts of boring ways. Watching us drink our coffee together in the morning from their windows, reading books, taking out the recycling, talking in English, which they don't understand. Our temporary kitchen is bigger than any other in the places

I've stayed and it's well-equipped. The refrigerator is full-sized, the espresso machine worthy of any restaurant. There's a terrace spanning one entire wall filling the white room with sunshine. The tiles are clean. There are two washrooms.

And I'm miserable. I'm disappointed. In this apartment and in all of us. We've been together for two days only and already I'm just so disappointed. It's not the apartment, not really. It's not Rome because we haven't had a chance to see Rome yet. We're still in our own heads thinking about other places. I'm thinking of Nick and thinking it's just two more weeks of only seeing him on FaceTime. I don't know where the kids are in their brains, but I know they're not here. They're together, that's for sure. But wherever they are, this place isn't available to me.

I forgot this. I forgot in the last four months when I pined for them that sometimes I might not like them very much at all. When I planned our trip together, I didn't see past the point of getting them here, not really. The group of us all in Europe together was as far as I could get in my imagination. I just wanted them to get here with me.

I'll tell you, I thought they'd be grateful. I thought they'd be in awe that finally I could do something for them that was a real moment. Every time I booked a flight or reminded someone to get their passport renewed or sent yet another link to yet another apartment or house for them to look at, I thought they'd be sort of amazed by me. That this woman who used to plan their birthday parties one month after their birthdays so she could afford to give their friends cake *and* ice cream, who sometimes gave a card with a note about what they could expect for their birthday once she got paid on Friday, this time she finally, finally, finally came through for them. And what's more, she grew all of a sudden. Instead of becoming a person who couldn't breathe without them, this woman who was their mother tried to find a path where she could let them breathe too. I thought they knew how hard this was. I thought they understood.

In Paris, I saw glimpses of something in them, an understanding let's call it. When we walked around Montmartre just before midnight, wandering from wine bar to wine bar, talking about our old lives and our new lives and all the plans they had for themselves that are not my stories to share but instead to hold, there was a glimmer. A connection. We ate crepes from a street vendor, thin layers of light batter wrapped around strawberry preserves or chocolate or apricot jelly served hot in a pouch. We shared our food as we walked. And when we walked back down to our hostel for the night, the stairs were lit in such a way that we all recognized, we were in a movie moment. "I think these are the stairs from *Midnight in Paris*, right?" Jessica asked and we were all pretty sure she was right.

That night I slept in the same room as three of my boys for the first time in forever. Their breathing sounded the same when they slept as it did when they were boys. Jack mumbling in his sleep, Cal with his soft whistle when he exhales sometimes, Nathan making no sound at all. Not a whisper. I slept a little that night but mostly, mostly I listened to them being with me.

The flight from Paris to Rome wasn't a good one. It was short but uncomfortable, made more so by a scuffle over Callum's bag with a flight attendant who said it was too big for a carry-on. I tried to help him because the attendant insisted he pay €150, and the look of terror on Cal's face told me he didn't have it, but I was pushed aside. Jessica, fierce and bilingual and not so easily pushed aside, cleared it up. Callum didn't have to pay, but the damage was done to us all. The mood shifted. The mood shifted away from me.

There is this thing my boys have done for years when they're together that I mostly love but sometimes hate. They band together, they close the circle and leave me on the outside in a way where I'm always meant to be aware I'm on the outside. This sounds ridiculous coming from a mother and I hear it in myself, but it hurts, my God, it hurts. It hurts because my job as a parent sometimes is to be the least popular person in the room and pretend like it's my absolute favourite thing, but it isn't.

It started on the day we left Paris, in Le Marché aux Puces de Saint-Ouen, one of the most famous flea markets in the city. I wanted to see it and the kids all said they'd come along, but on the walk, I could see this wasn't what they wanted. They whispered to each other and laughed and had a generally good time together. Or if they were unhappy with me, they'd exchange looks with each other just as I was turning my head, just in time for me to catch them before their faces went blank again.

The walk to Les Puces took us through some neighbourhoods that were a bit unfortunate, lots of big-block apartment buildings and laundromats with the doors wedged open. Jack found the flea market eventually, but at first blush it was a disappointment. Vendors selling bundles of tube socks and knockoff perfumes. A lot of aggressive yelling, a lot of cars honking close to the highway. I could feel the boys behind me rolling their eyes. I could feel them saying, *Why does she always drag us to these places?* I could feel my face getting red, my ears getting hot, my day going down the tubes. The flea market turned out to be incredible once we got to the inner sanctum. But it wasn't enough to save the day. I couldn't see the vintage dresses or the delicate china or the pre-war trinkets. I couldn't get past feeling alone with these people I'd waited for. The same people who hung back to talk together, away from me but within sight, who looked, for all the world, like the same little boys I used to bring to the grocery store, arms crossed militantly in the checkout lane.

By the time we get to Rome, I'm lost. I feel lost. As though the last four months haven't happened.

I look in the mirror in the bathroom and try to see a bit of the person I've become. A woman who made friends without her kids, without the mom qualifier I secretly suspect I might always need. She came to me quietly but is gone now. She's a ghost. The woman that looks back at me needs to get to the supermarket before it closes to pick up a few things for breakfast. She needs to stop feeling so goddamn sorry for herself and organize something for a late dinner. Outside the bathroom door awaits that old hunger that won't ever, ever be satisfied, and this is her job. She needs to remind one boy to buy himself some new shoes and give another boy some toothpaste. She needs to wrap her head around sleeping in the same room with Jack since Ben and Jessica need the double bed with the ensuite (that she booked for herself). But no, this isn't going to happen. Instead it's a single bed in a child's bedroom with her grown son at the other end. This woman forgot in the past four months that she used to live in a box labelled "mother" and nothing more. Her sons don't want to hear her speaking Italian or French or see her wearing red lipstick, they want her back in the box, back in the bleachers cheering them on. This is what the other mothers are doing, and it should be noted, the other mothers are doing this without complaint. This woman was given four months to be someone else, and that's more than most get. It's time to climb back into that box. To smile ruefully when the boys roll their eyes or worse, when they stop listening and slide their eyes to their phones halfway through a story. To have actual answers for the questions they ask, which are always exactly the same: *What's for breakfast? What's for lunch? What's for dinner? Do we have snacks in the fridge? Can we get takeout? Is there anything to drink other than water?* And on and on and on. I like this box a lot, mostly. But I think maybe it needs some renovating.

Everyone is standing in the kitchen when I walk in with my speech. It's dark outside, maybe around eight o'clock. Jessica stands by the kitchen window and I'm sorry to say she gets cornered by me and my sons. I say to them, "Do you know how lonely I've been? For four months I've been alone. But not once did I feel more alone than I do with all of you here right now. It's like you all want to put me back in some fucking box where I'm just a mom, and you know what? No." I look at Jessica for a second to apologize. She's nodding along with me, eyebrows raised in that way like, yup. I've never loved her more.

I say, "I don't expect you to fall down at my feet but here's what I do expect. I expect you to thank me. This was hard for me to save up for and to plan, and not one of you have said thank you, not once. So that every time you bitch and complain about the flights or the cost of food or the walking or the language barrier, it's not even like I get a baseline of gratitude from you. And it really sucks."

The boys are ready to fight. Ready to defend themselves with their numbers and with the knowledge that I love them so much. So much, even in that moment. But I turn and walk out of the room. They leave. Jessica too. They tell me later that they found a little bar a few doors down and went to have a drink there. They tell me it was fine, so I shouldn't feel bad. Because at first, they thought I should feel bad.

I watch a movie on Netflix but don't see a minute of it. I cry. For an hour I cry. My God, I am so tired of crying, so bored with my tears, but here they come anyhow. They come for the trip I thought we'd have. For twenty-five years of wanting something and not knowing why but knowing deep down, this isn't the thing I'm going to get. Not here, maybe not ever.

But I found things too. I don't want to forget this. I found a bottle of red wine in the cupboard from the landlady as a welcome gift. I called Nick and told him I love him. I didn't tell him that my life with him was the one I was coming home to, but I think he knew. I think he could guess.

When everyone comes back to the apartment, I pretend to be asleep. Jack comes creeping into the room. He whispers, "Good night." I lie in the dark, listening to his breathing. His soft mumbles. It sounds as sweet as ever to me.

Ciao Roma

Rome opened up to me or I opened up to Rome. I didn't want to come back, not so soon after those first two months. But the boys wanted to see Rome, and so we came. And I'm so glad we did because Rome lays itself bare at my feet this time.

I told everyone about Rome. In France and Ireland, I moved from story to story about Italy that all ended the same way — "Yes, but…" Yes, Rome is beautiful, but the people wouldn't embrace me. Yes, it's the eternal city, but for me it was like standing and breathing on plate glass that separated me from everyone else. Yes, all Italians aren't the same, but let me tell you, it feels like they're all male and all tired of dealing with me. This I knew for sure.

Now Italy is different. The kids and I take the bus and then the Metro into the city centre, and I'm easy with it. At the bus stop, a woman asks me if the 980 bus had already been by, and I sit in that for a moment because this means she thinks I'm a local. My Italian is restaurant-proficient when we go to lunch at a little pizzeria close to the Pantheon and even supermarket-advanced when we shop for groceries. When a woman says to me, "*Dire me, cara,*" I can tell her the exact kind of fruit I want to buy, and she finds it for me. I learn to apologize for my terrible Italian in pretty great-sounding Italian, and when I do this, every time the person says to me, "No, you are amazing, your accent is perfect." They say this, I suppose, because we're all friends here now. The boys remain indifferent to my Italian accent. As a group they look away when I ask for something in Italian, like they can't hear me or won't hear me. They aren't, however, indifferent to Rome itself.

After our first night in Rome, we come to an agreement that no one says out loud. After they find a pizza place where they could have a drink together and talk about things, and I have a few hours to think about things. We decide that I have to let it all go. The picture, the twenty-five years, the dreams of being better and best and together. It'll all come to ruin if I don't let it go. And fast. I don't want to let it all go, and I'm not even all that sure of what I'm letting go, but this is the thing that has to be done.

I have to let go of my big ending. For four months plus twenty-five years or so, I thought about what this end of the trip would look like. Two weeks in Europe with my kids, a graduation present for us all together. Time. I wasn't always sure if our trip would be in a villa in France where we'd take our meals outside on a porch dripping with climbing grape vines or maybe a beach hut in Hawaii or even for a while I thought I could maybe get us all to Bali. I'd give them time together and time with me. I thought this trip would be a coming-of-age kind of thing for all of us, but now I see what it really might be, an apology tour. A way for me to wipe the slate clean. I hoped they would all remember my strong finish as a mom more than my dismal beginnings and mediocre middle. But the slate can't be wiped clean. They don't say this, but I see pretty quickly, it isn't going to be wiped clean.

When they come back that first night, I think they feel a little bit sorry for making me cry but mostly I think they feel resentful. I don't ask them if this trip is what they wanted. I tell them it's what they wanted. No. I tell them this is what *I* wanted. And I don't allow them to say no. No one allows them to say no. I paid for a trip that I forced them to take and I expected them to fall down at my feet in gratitude. Everyone expected this, every friend and relative. And I think maybe this is how they felt growing up with a single mom. Forced to say thank you for something they didn't always want and certainly hadn't chosen. My mom telling them as little boys, "You're so lucky to have a mom who loves you," like they owed me. Teachers telling me (in front of their faces) that I was doing such a good job with "all those boys, my God," the subtext always *that poor woman with all those boys*. Every restaurant, every store, every supermarket. Always a note of pity. "Your grocery bills must be ridiculous" and "I bet you can't wait until they finally leave." As though my boys were unable to understand words in plain English. As though they should know they were nothing but a burden to me.

When I wake up that first morning in Rome, the sun is shining. Everyone is awake but quiet. Quiet and looking at the floor, at the wall, at their phones. Anywhere but at me or each other. Wondering what I will do.

I look at them then and just like that, I let it go. "Who wants coffee? I don't know how to use this espresso machine, so I'll go to the café by the bus stop." Their relief is everywhere. It's climbing the walls. They all offer to come with me, they all offer to pay for the coffee. I go alone, but before I leave, I say, "I don't want to waste this time being mad because I wanted it to be different. Let's just try to think

of what everyone wants to do and figure it out from there."
And so, we do.

Callum doesn't want to join everything all the time. And
so, he cooks dinners. He's so passionate about the food in
Italy. Every night he makes us amazing pasta, great bowls of
it on the middle of the table. Every second day he comes
touring around with us, but I give him his space. Nathan stays
with him, always the youngest boy. Always wanting to be
with Callum since he was a toddler and maybe even before.
Ben and Jessica want a few days to explore on their own. Jack
has a list of pizza places he wants to try. He wants to see the
Colosseum. He wants to do everything. And in this way, he
becomes my constant companion in Italy. The boy by my side
with his good camera, his backpack, his Google Maps. He
becomes the photographer for us all when we visit the
Colosseum, and the boys are quiet with the heavy ghosts they
feel there. When we stand inside the Pantheon, and it rains
through the oculus. When we visit all the places I've seen
before, I have to stop myself from watching them, from
wanting them to delight in everything. I have to stop myself
from thinking they owe me their delight.

The money issue is difficult, maybe it will always be
difficult. I can't pay for anyone because then I'd have to pay
for everyone. The only way around this is our morning
coffees from the little café and groceries. I can still afford to
pay a bit extra for groceries, but there remains a constant
twist in my stomach when any of the kids has to spend
money, when I have a rough idea of every boy's bank
account and watch the numbers get smaller and smaller
with every gelato, every slice of pizza, every train ride or bus
fare. My money is running out. It has run out. I live on
borrowed money from Nick now, Nick who's at home fixing

my car in his driveway after having it towed to his house, trying not to complain even though all he wants to do is complain. Mostly he just wants me to come home. The complaining can come later.

Our dinners are perhaps my favourite. Fresh pasta with vegetables, and we set the table and drink wine together after a day of wandering. There's bread in the shape of rosettes pulled apart with sweet Italian butter. Dinner takes hours. The dishes are done in shifts and then everyone goes back to the table to play Pictionary or cards or talk and talk with music in the background. Sometimes I have this mean little pouty thought. *We could be doing this in Canada just the same*, but I let it go.

I just keep on letting it go.

A few days in, we decide to take the train to the sea, to a little village called Santa Marinella. The train takes an hour and on the way we talk about weddings. People sometimes think that with boys, this never comes up in their heads at all. But it does and they do. In Santa Marinella, we walked the beach after eating more pizza that's only average. The boys are becoming snobs about pizza by this point, and everyone's favourite seems to be the local joint near the apartment, the eggplant pizza especially, extra Parmesan. The beach in Santa Marinella is warm, warm enough for some of the boys to strip off their t-shirts. Warm enough that we buy some wine and beer and sit on the boardwalk with our feet up, having a drink and discussing our lives so far.

I learn from Ben that everyone is so grateful for this trip. Nathan talks and talks about Ireland then. About how much fun we had. About how friendly people were, about how we hiked and hiked. I didn't know we had fun until he told his brothers.

I learn from Jack that he might not say I'm a great mom, but he's always thought I was a great mom. I'm always going to be one of his people, even though he's so different from me with his lists and organization and ambition for a future where he doesn't get a pit in his stomach over money, even in middle age. Not like me. Jack has certain people in his circle and once you're there you'll always be there. He's discerning about his people and if you aren't one of them, you'll have no mercy from him. I'm one of his people. For good. He let me know this today.

Callum talks about pizza. He talks about it like it's a living, breathing thing because maybe it is for him. He talks about how Italy has opened his eyes to his passion for food. About how he might want to make pizza for a living. We all say we love this idea so many times that he believes us. He still believes us because this is true.

On the train back from Santa Marinella, our skin is hot and tight from the sun. The scenery is sun-faded small villages and the bright-blue sea everywhere. Some people sleep, others whisper, still others put in their headphones to listen to music. Our bellies are full of gelato and pizza. Our minds are full of all of the hopeful secret stories we told each other. This is what I came for.

Two days before we fly home, Luca arranges for all of us to go to San Polo dei Cavalieri for lunch so he and Angela can meet the boys. He makes a reservation at Il Braciere, and so we go in two cars up to the mountaintop village. It's Mother's Day. We're going to lunch in a village in Italy for Mother's Day. After, we'll walk around Tivoli. I'll show them the apartment where I stayed. Show them the town. I'll see the town for myself again.

Luca and Angela book us the entire lower level of the restaurant. It looks as if it was a wine cellar at some point, one long table with a view of the valley from the windows and the terrace outside. Stone walls that are cool to the touch, a breeze through the screen windows. The owner kisses me when she see me, both cheeks and hands. The boys look nervous at first, but Luca solves this problem immediately. "Drink the wine, we'll all be more charming," he tells them. And so, they do. Even Nathan, who doesn't really drink. Given the choice between nervously trying to speak Italian or drinking wine he chooses the wine. Conversation is difficult at first, but once the food starts to arrive, people relax. Plate after plate of bread and pasta and vegetables and cheese. Passed around with sounds that translate to joy instead of words in any language.

I sit at the head of the table and Luca keeps making a joke out of it, the "top of the pyramid," "nobody is above Jennifer," and more. He does this for the boys, and I love him for it. Angela is quiet, nervous, I assume, about her English. She smiles at the boys and tells me they are so handsome. She says, "Beautiful, beautiful family," and I think she's surprised by this. I think it was hard for her to imagine me as a mom even though I talked about the kids all the time. I think about how I now have friends in the world who only know me as me. How impossible that still seems. How my few friends in Italy and France and Ireland know me. The real me. And how I think I can exist without the boys now. I wear some red lipstick to lunch at Il Braciere, the only lipstick I own. Angela gestures to it and says, "This is new." It's all new. Things can still be new.

The lunch comes to an end after two or three hours, I don't know for sure. Nathan drinks wine with us all and loosens, Luca telling me that "he is like a movie star." We walk to my old little studio in Tivoli after. The American couple staying inside hears our voices and opens the tiny window in the door and says, "Do I hear American out there?" They invite us in to see the place and it looks the same to me. Lonely. The couple are baby boomers who say they're travelling around Europe as millennials might. The husband hopes his blog will take off and asks me for contacts when one of the boys lets slip that I'm a writer. He's arrogant in the way older white men can sometimes be and I'm glad to leave him. I'm glad to leave the wife too, though I feel sorry for her. She's huddled on my old bed in layers of cotton-cashmere blend, complaining about the unfriendliness of the people in Tivoli, the cold drafty cave of a room, the distance from Rome. She's the ghost of the woman I used to be. Not ready to be happy yet. Not ready to stop feeling so alone. Nathan says to me in his wine-drunk voice after we leave, "No wonder you felt sad there. That place was crazy depressing."

I take them to the courtyard around the corner, where the stray cats come out as the sun goes down and people bring them dishes of tuna. I take them to the gates of Villa Gregoriana. I show them the waterfalls, the sparkling fountain of fresh, cold water and the grocery store where I couldn't make myself understood.

When we leave for the train, Luca kisses my cheeks and I nearly cry. The last time we said goodbye, he and Angela and I were coming back from a weekend in L'Aquila in the Abruzzo region. The town that was levelled by an earthquake in 2009 and is still rebuilding. His parents had an apartment there and we spent my last weekend together before I left for Avignon. It was a strange weekend. Angela was very sick with a cold and she wished she didn't have to host me then. She didn't want to come up with English words, she wanted to fight with Luca in their own Italian and eat leftovers and sleep. Luca and I tried to hike in the mountains close by, up to Rocca Calascio where they filmed *Ladyhawke* (he kept telling me even though I had no memory of this movie at all), but the snow was too thick for us. We ate hot soup and thick bread at a place called La Taberna that looked like a ski chalet, stone walls and rounded doors and a roaring fire. That weekend, we walked and ate and said goodbye without saying goodbye. When the time came to say goodbye the first time around, I wanted to tell Luca and Angela that they sort of saved me. Luca saved me with hikes and, yes, even that one time when we went to karaoke for his friend's birthday and they sang "Tu Vuo' Fa' L'Americano" and did choreographed dancing. Angela saved me by taking me to her stylist and showing me how I could eat my food without shame. I wanted to tell them thank you but all we had time for was, "Okay, ciao!" because they dropped me off at the curb close to my house.

This time the goodbye isn't a practice. Things have shifted over the past few months. We're different to each other now. Kisses on the cheek and a "see you soon." Luca and I won't see each other soon. We know this. But there's no saying this now.

On Monday the kids and I are flying to Paris then home, most of us. Jessica and Ben are heading off to wander around Austria and Germany and northern France by themselves. We stay up late on Sunday talking and wake up early to clean the apartment. Nobody wants to see the landlady again or any of her relatives.

There are no tears when we leave Rome. I don't cry when I walk Ben and Jessica to the bus stop, and I don't cry when Jack and Cal have to hop on a separate flight from Paris back to Toronto. *They aren't lost to me* — this is the only lesson I really learned there. They aren't the same boys, and I won't ever get them back, not even for a weekend visit. The two-year-old versions of my sons are dead and buried forever. Forever. Forever. But now I think I like these people too. I like them almost better than anybody.

Almost.

May Peepers

In Canada it's warm and I'm grateful for it. This is something I missed, the warmth after months of cold. The change in our air. Nathan and I get back to the stone house in Annan around seven o'clock. Nick is on my doorstep by 7:15. I run to him or I run at him.

If you ever want to really know how you feel about a person, stand real still and quiet in the hoop of their arms for five seconds and then ten seconds. I know how I feel now. Nick cries and I cry, but his tears, he tells me after, are mostly relief. "I've gotten so old," he tells me. "I thought you would feel different when you saw me." He isn't so old to me.

I leave Nathan in Annan with some food. We're ready to be apart for a night, and even if we both aren't ready, I'm ready.

It's a Tuesday. I have to work first thing in the morning, but I just want to be with Nick at the log cabin in the woods for a night. He makes dinner for me. The next day, I don't remember what we ate. Instead, I remember just him. Just my relief that we are still these people to each other. That we didn't lose something in those months. That he's still mine and I'm still his. Even if I don't know what that means for what we'll do next. At least I know this. Nick isn't nervous with me and I'm not nervous with him.

That night I lie in his bed in his arms in his sheets, naked, one leg kicked outside of the duvet. I'm only ever naked with Nick. The windows are open. I hear the peepers outside. I sleep so deep I might not be breathing at all. Canada.

In the morning, I brush my teeth in Nick's washroom over his sink.

There's toothpaste spit on the mirror.